Praise for *52 Things Wives Need from Their Husbands*

"A realistic (and humorous) look at married life and how husbands can use their strengths to celebrate and lift up their wives. I wish I'd had this book years ago—it would have saved me a lot of apologizing!"

—**Rick Johnson,** bestselling author of
Becoming Your Spouse's Better Half and *Better Dads, Stronger Sons*

"Every man needs what this book's got! Practical, simple ideas on how to love your wife. Give it a try!"

—**Dan Seaborn,** president, Winning at Home

"Helping men connect with their wives is a huge way to strengthen families. Once again Jay has provided a wealth of great ideas husbands can put into action."

Carey Casey, CEO of The National Center for Fathering,
radio host, and author of *Championship Fathering*

"I read Jay's book...nodded my head and smiled...wondered how he got so smart about women...and decided to get a copy for my husband and each of our three married sons!...Thank you, Jay, from all the women whose husbands will read this book."

Kendra Smiley, speaker,
author of *Do Your Kids a Favor...Love Your Spouse*

"Are you taking your wife for granted? That girl you married needs you! And you need her!...Jay's book is a timely reminder for men that marriage is an awesome gift from God."

—**Darrel Billups,** executive director of
the National Coalition of Ministries to Men (NCMM)

"Wives, watch out. You are about to be loved, cherished, and surprised!"

—**Josh McDowell,** author and international speaker

"When your wife 'rises up and calls you blessed,' you'll owe Jay Payleitner for having written this book. Every father and husband ought to read, underline, and live it."

—**Steve Brown,** popular author,
or, and radio teacher on Key Life

Positive words for Jay's previous book
52 Things Kids Need from a Dad

"Every dad will see himself in the funny and enlightening pages of this book—an excellent choice for any man who is or expects to be a father."

—CBA Retailers + Resources

"This is great stuff, worth any dad's time. If you can't benefit from this, you're not listening. Ignore it only if you don't want to be a better dad. The first three copies are going to my grown sons."

—Jerry B. Jenkins, coauthor of the megaselling Left Behind series
and author of over 150 other published works

"By offering such varied topics, Payleitner gives fathers a well-rounded view of what children need in an accessible format. Whether you're just starting out as a father or partway through the journey of raising your children, you'll find fresh ideas."

—MetroChristianLiving.com

"I highly recommend this book to all dads. It is a good read and, more importantly, a great guide for any man desiring to meet the needs of the children God has entrusted to his care."

—Kendra Smiley, radio host, conference speaker,
and author of *Be the Parent* and *High-Wire Mom*

"Moms of all ages, grab this book for your husbands! It's inspiring, encouraging, and easy to read."

—Ellen Banks Elwell, author of *The Christian Mom's Idea Book*
and *When There's Not Enough of Me to Go Around*

"You won't find any lectures or guilt trips here. Instead, it's more like 52 inspiring halftime talks. As your personal fathering coach, Jay will provoke you to think deep, laugh hard, and love more, leaving you with 52 unexpected fathering insights."

—Carey Casey, CEO of The National Center for Fathering,
speaker, radio host, and author of *Championship Fathering*

52 THINGS WIVES NEED
FROM THEIR
HUSBANDS

JAY PAYLEITNER

HARVEST HOUSE PUBLISHERS
EUGENE, OREGON

All Scripture quotations, unless otherwise indicated, are taken from The Holy Bible, *New International Version*® *NIV*®. Copyright © 1973, 1978, 1984, 2011 by Biblica, Inc.™ Used by permission. All rights reserved worldwide. Or from The Holy Bible, *New International Version*® *NIV*®. Copyright © 1973, 1978, 1984 by Biblica, Inc.™ Used by permission. All rights reserved worldwide.

Verses marked NLT are taken from the Holy Bible, New Living Translation, copyright © 1996, 2004. Used by permission of Tyndale House Publishers, Inc., Wheaton, IL 60189 USA. All rights reserved.

Verses marked NASB are taken from the New American Standard Bible ®, © 1960, 1962, 1963, 1968, 1971, 1972, 1973, 1975, 1977, 1995 by The Lockman Foundation. Used by permission. (www.Lockman.org)

Cover by e210 Design, Eagan, Minnesota

Cover photo © Jupiterimages / Brand X Pictures / Getty

Jay Payleitner is represented by MacGregor Literary, Inc., of Hillsboro, Oregon.

52 THINGS WIVES NEED FROM THEIR HUSBANDS
Copyright © 2011 by Jay K. Payleitner
Published by Harvest House Publishers
Eugene, Oregon 97402
www.harvesthousepublishers.com

Library of Congress Cataloging-in-Publication Data

Payleitner, Jay K.
    52 things wives need from their husbands / Jay Payleitner.
        p. cm.
    ISBN 978-0-7369-4471-7 (pbk.)
    ISBN 978-0-7369-4427-4 (eBook)
    1. Marriage. 2. Marriage—Religious aspects—Christianity. 3. Husbands—Conduct of life.
4. Wives—Psychology. I. Title. II. Title: Fifty-two things wives need from their husbands.
    HQ734.P317 2011
    248.8'44—dc23

                                                                                    2011025582

All rights reserved. No part of this publication may be reproduced, stored in a retrieval system, or transmitted in any form or by any means—electronic, mechanical, digital, photocopy, recording, or any other—except for brief quotations in printed reviews, without the prior permission of the publisher.

Printed in the United States of America

12 13 14 15 16 17 18 19 / VP-SK / 10 9 8 7 6 5 4 3

To my parents, who modeled marriage done well
for more than 60 years.
I love you. Thanks.

Acknowledgments

After finishing this manuscript, but before it went to press, I lost my dad to bone and liver cancer. Since this page is set aside for acknowledgments, I'd like to acknowledge him. Ever so briefly.

As I am the writer in the family, the task of crafting my father's obituary fell to me, which turned out to be a puzzle and a privilege. At the very least, it made me think about what my own kids might write about me someday.

Ken Payleitner was an elementary-school principal for 32 years. In the weeks since he passed, I've heard stories from dozens of former students and teachers about his compassion, open-door policy, and kid-friendly approach to education. Those firsthand recollections were good to hear. It's satisfying to think that his impact on real lives continues.

Dad was one of the few remaining World War II vets, a skilled carpenter, a tree planter, a fisherman, and a diehard Cubs fan. He desperately loved his four kids, eleven grandchildren, two great-grandchildren, and my mom—his bride of more than 60 years. He was also an excellent father-in-law, which is no small thing. His legacy is firmly in place.

I loved him a lot and he knew it. When I was a boy, he was an involved dad, which I did not fully appreciate until much later. Still, it was the conversations I had with him over the last decade that will stick with me most. Dialogues about spiritual truths and the meaning of life. We were both lifelong learners.

The idea of being married six decades should not be a big deal. The formula is simple. Get married in your 20s and live into your 80s. What's tough about that? You get out of bed for 22,000 mornings in a row, brush your teeth, kiss your wife, and do the work God puts in front of you. My dad lived the biblical instruction, "Whatever your hand finds to do, do it with all your might" (Ecclesiastes 9:10).

In the light of eternity, I'm pretty sure I can do that for a mere 60 years. I'm thinking you can, too.

Other acknowledgments for this page include the usual suspects at Harvest House, my agent, my family and friends, guys in my small group, and pastors who have invited me to come speak to their men's group. We're all in this together.

And thanks again, Dad. I'll see you soon.

Contents

Foreword
by Angela Thomas

I f I had written this book's foreword 30 naïve years ago, I might have wanted to add 152 *more* things wives need from their husbands. But brokenness has this beautiful way of reshaping the heart if you'll let it. I was married, divorced, lived seven years as a single mom to four children, and then remarried a little over three years ago. My journey in marriage was difficult, broken, and lonely. Then there was a long season of healing, eventually redemption, and now, oh hallelujah, marriage for me is sweet love.

Today, I write to you realizing I don't need very much from my husband. My list is pretty short these days. Though Jay has covered so many great ideas in the pages ahead, I'll give you my top three. I need my husband to...

1. obey God
2. live gratefully
3. be nice

All the little things that seem so important become minuscule when you wake up beside a kind, happy person who loves God. I have the great privilege of being married to Scott Pharr. His obedience to God covers everything I could ever desire my husband to be. And from that obedience, his consistent kindness and joy has created a gracious home of peace and laughter for our children and me.

It's so amazing how kindness diminishes the differences, the shortcomings, and the flat-out mistakes—not only in our marriage, but in our parenting as well. When the man you love has chosen to wake up happy, then every day is a new beginning. A fresh start. An adventure to be lived.

Nearly everyone has known some degree of brokenness in their marriage journey too. Here's what I know: Brokenness can make you better. Truly. My husband and I love each other with a new, grateful love because we have both been desperately broken people. No matter what your marriage story has been, I pray that these pages will give new focus to your heart and fresh inspiration for you to love with freedom and grace.

Jay Payleitner offers great wit and wisdom in his writing, so I hope you'll let these 52 things do their work in your marriage…maybe even wake you up to some things you may have let slide.

I'm going to take the liberty of speaking on behalf of all the wives who will benefit so immensely from these pages. From the bottom of our hearts, thank you. Thank you for holding this book in your hands and reading its words. Even if you just scan a page or two from *52 Things Wives Need from their Husbands,* somebody should buy you a new golf club or take you hunting or something incredibly cool just to tell you how wonderful it is when a husband cares enough to read a book like this.

Blessings, my friend. Hug your wife a little longer than you used to. She needs it. Kiss her extra. She'll love it. As you read, look up every once in a while and tell her something you just discovered about what she needs. She'll get down on her knees and thank God for a man who wants to keep learning how to love her more.

Angela Thomas
Bestselling author and speaker

The 50/50 Marriage

Before I reveal the formula for living happily ever after, let's consider the work that needs to be done.

Bringing home a paycheck. Paying bills. Changing lightbulbs. Changing diapers. Grocery shopping. Making dinner. Making lunches. Remembering birthdays. Tucking in. Weed whacking. Scheduling date nights. Carpooling to soccer. Planning vacations. Planning retirement. Feeding the dog. Waiting for the cable guy. Assembling furniture from Ikea. Sorting socks. Signing report cards. Entertaining in-laws. Running out for milk. Loading the dishwasher. Laundry. Taxes. Romance. Etcetera.

Over the years, these tasks will somehow be divided into "his," "hers," "both," and "whoever is available at the time."

When the dust settles, your day-to-day list of responsibilities may have a sense of balance. You do the tucking in. She makes lunches. You run out for milk. She feeds the dog. You dirty dishes. She washes dishes.

Gentlemen, this is the first big takeaway of this book: *Never suggest or even think that marriage is a 50/50 proposition.* You will lose that argument.

Yes, I know you pull your own weight. I believe you do more than the average schmuck when it comes to daily housekeeping chores. Plus, if you and your wife logged and compared hours spent on home repairs and maintenance, you would win hands-down. And those hands would display some well-earned, oil, sweat, and blood.

But come on. I am not trying to make you feel guilty, but you and I both know she does more of the tedious day-to-day tasks than you.

There's an old joke that says it well. "When a woman says she's going to bed, she wipes down the counters, loads and starts the dishwasher, preps the coffeemaker for the morning, moves a load of clothes from the washer to the dryer, locks the doors, checks on the sleeping babies, turns out the lights, brushes her teeth, sets the alarm clock, and goes to bed. When a man says he's going to bed, he turns off the TV and goes to bed."

A slight exaggeration? Maybe. But trust me. Keeping track of who pulls more weight during the course of the day or week is not the recipe for a healthy marriage. I'm begging you not to play the game, "If I do this for her, she'll do this for me." It's a never-ending tug of war pitting husband against wife. How can that be a good thing?

Once you move beyond the typical day-to-day routine, the 50/50 idea becomes even more problematic. Season to season, the give and take of a marriage relationship can teeter-totter drastically.

There are all kinds of life events that happen to a wife or a husband as individuals. Job loss. Job promotion. Volunteer opportunities. Change of career. A friend moves away. A parent dies. Pregnancy. Midlife crisis. Menopause. Impotence. Illness. Disability. These things initially impact one of you, but ripple quickly to your spouse and the rest of the family.

There are also things—good and bad—that impact both a husband and wife simultaneously. Moving across town. Moving across the country. A financial setback or windfall. Loss of a child. Difficulty conceiving. Changing churches. Some kind of natural disaster. A child heads off to college, joins the military, or gets married. As a couple, these things happen to both of you, but often hit one of you harder than the other.

Over the decades, it becomes very clear. Life is not 50/50.

And that is one of the very best arguments in favor of marriage.

Husbands and wives share life. We carry each other. We celebrate and console. We love each other unconditionally through the sunny days and rainy nights. We help each other stay grounded even as we encourage each other to reach new heights. We give. We receive.

If you stick with it, somewhere along the way every couple will discover the fairy-tale formula for marriage. It's 100/100.

I'm not sure about the math. But I'm sure that Rita and I have been working our way toward those numbers for more than 30 years. It's worth the effort. You'll see.

"True love begins when nothing is looked for in return."
Antoine de Saint-Exupéry (1900–1944)

Wives Need Their Husbands…

To Kiss the Girl

A husband and wife are driving down a country road. They're a few years older than you are now. He's behind the wheel. The pavement and cornfields are passing by. She breaks the silence with a sigh and says, "Remember when we were younger and we used to sit right next to each other in the car?" "I remember," the husband replies after a moment. "But you know, I haven't moved."

It's a story from way before seat-belt laws, but the sentiment still carries a bushel of truth. Men—the good ones like you and me—travel down the road of life with a sense of stability and direction. We're not out drinking every night. We do our best to bring home a paycheck and be a good father. An affair is not an option. Neither is divorce. Our deepest need is for our bride to sit close to us and tell us—just once in a while—that we're doing a good job. That we're appreciated. That they look up to us and need us.

Our wives, on the other hand, slide back and forth. Like many women these days, they are getting mixed messages and giving mixed signals. They don't seem to know what they want. A career or a houseful of babies? A new washer/dryer or a week in Aruba? A bigger house or just bigger closets? Do they want a husband who is sensitive and tender or a tattooed bad boy riding a Harley? While they're daydreaming about what they want, we're just two feet away and hoping they'll ask us for it. We want to fill their every desire. We want to be their shining knight and perfect man. If only they'd slide next to us and tell us what they want.

How did we get here? Two feet and two miles apart.

Think back to not too long ago. Remember that girl you married? The girl who caught your eye. The girl you couldn't keep your hands off of. The girl who taught you to love in brand-new ways. Romantic love. Committed love. Crazy love. Eternal love. Silly love. You may be thinking, *Where did that girl go?*

Gentlemen, she's right there. That girl is inches away. She's looking down the same road and going the same direction. She's committed to sharing your life and sharing your bed. By the way, she's asking the same question. *Where did that boy go?*

Men of courage, follow your impulse. Pull the car over. Look into her eyes, maybe for the first time in a long time. Tell her she means everything to you. Be the boy. Be the girl. Expect no less than to memorize each other's hopes and dreams.

Steam up those car windows. With conversation, of course.

Takeaway

You did not marry to live separate lives.

> *"Love is as strong as death, its jealousy unyielding as the grave. It burns like blazing fire, like a mighty flame. Many waters cannot quench love; rivers cannot sweep it away."*
>
> Song of Songs 8:6-7

Wives Need Their Husbands...

To Push the Right Buttons

H ere are some things my bride likes: fireworks, parades, a company bathroom that's welcoming, babies, cute babies, goofy-looking babies, well-produced television commercials with cute or goofy-looking babies, scones, sparkly glassware on her Thanksgiving dinner table, hanging out with her children, bling for Christmas, warm feet, lying on a beach with a book, fresh flowers, fresh snow, frozen Cokes, lightly buttered popcorn, drinking straws, craft magazines, etcetera.

It's a good list. And I'll probably think of a few more things in the normal course of life. I'll have to make sure my editor checks with me right before going to press to see if there are a few more things to add. Actually, just writing this list has been a valuable exercise. Thinking about what my bride likes literally strengthens my marriage.

A couple of things worth noting about this kind of list. It focuses on the positive. I could have included items such as "chili that's not filled with cayenne pepper" and "kitchen countertops without a bunch of appliances." But that would essentially be a list of things she doesn't like (spicy chili and cluttered counters). Everything on the list gives off mostly positive vibes. Of course, we husbands should be well aware of what our wives don't like, but that's not the point of this chapter.

The other thing about this list is that these are not emotional needs or love languages exclusive to the husband-wife relationship. These are things Rita likes anytime, anyplace, no matter who provides them. If a scone, fresh flowers, or craft magazine mysteriously appeared on our kitchen table, she would enjoy that thing simply because she likes it. Sure, part of the fun of parades and fireworks is sharing them with others, but I'm pretty sure Rita would enjoy them in the company of strangers.

You probably know where I'm going with this. A wise husband will make a similar list particular to his own wife. Using it and updating it frequently.

In random order, provide one of those items to your bride once a week for the rest of your life. Be intentional about it. Find a scone bakery on the way home from work. On movie night, make sure you have some microwave popcorn in the cabinet. Book a beach vacation.

Or better, keep the list at the top of your mind and allow it to trigger spontaneous moments when you provide your wife one of her favorite things. While you're waiting for a prescription, if you notice a craft magazine, pick it up. If one of those cute-baby commercials comes on when she's in the kitchen, pause the DVR and play it for her when she returns. If you notice the sun glinting off a fresh snowfall, stop what you're doing and share the moment with your bride.

The goal here is not selfish. It's easy to think, *If I give her what she likes, she'll give me what I like.* That's not it at all. The goal is to fully integrate into your marriage the "two becoming one" idea from Matthew chapter 19. Maybe think of it this way: *If I give her what she likes, it gives me joy as well.*

Making sense? No? It makes total sense to me, but perhaps that is because I started this chapter out with a list specific to my bride. I'm pretty sure that if you make a similar list for yours, it will all be clear. Don't just do it in your head. Get out a yellow pad or open a new Word doc and just start thinking about what makes your wife smile. Your mind may start to wander to the stuff that ticks her off or launches an unwelcome bout of nagging, but don't go there. Stay positive.

I promise, just making that list will give you all kinds of fresh insights, warm fuzzies, and a new appreciation for your bride. You'll begin to see her as only a devoted husband can. There are things you know about her that no one else does. Which means only you can intentionally and regularly provide those moments of joy. Only you can prompt that intimate smile that makes marriage different than any other relationship in the world.

Takeaway

The longer you're married, the more you know how to push your wife's buttons. Which ones to push and how often is really your choice.

*"Despite my thirty years of research into the feminine soul,
I have not been able to answer the great question that has
never been answered: What does a woman want?"*

SIGMUND FREUD (1856–1939)

Wives Need Their Husbands…

To Leave So You Can Cleave

I know you love your mom. She made you chicken soup when you were sniffly. She made sure your bath towels were fluffy. She cut the crusts off your peanut-butter-and-jelly "samwiches."

But you ain't married to her. The day you slipped that ring on your bride's finger, your sweet, devoted mother took a demotion. She became the number-two woman in your life. Furthermore, if you also happen to have a daughter or two, grandma is now number three or four. And if your son is married, then your daughter-in-law might even have passed your mother on the priority ranking.

If you're saying, "Of course I love my mom, but I have moved out and moved on," then feel free to skip the rest of this chapter. But for some reason, that is not the case with many husbands.

Why do some newly married men hang so tightly to their mom's apron strings? And why do moms let them? I am not going to quote Freud or refer to psychosexual oedipal issues. What I am going to say is, cut it out. Grow up. Today, you need to commit to building a new family with your bride, who wants to do that more than anything.

This idea is so important that it appears twice in the Bible in all but identical language. In Genesis, right after the creation of Adam and Eve, we get this clear instruction.

> That is why a man leaves his father and mother and is united to
> his wife, and they become one flesh (Genesis 2:24).

In the New Testament, Paul's letter to the Ephesians reminds husbands once again.

For this reason a man will leave his father and mother and be united to his wife, and the two will become one flesh (Ephesians 5:31).

Gentlemen, your wife needs to know you value her more than you value your own mother. She needs to know you have left your boyhood home and are building a new one with your name and hers on the mailbox. In very specific terms, leave and cleave. More than a clever rhyme, it's a biblically sound mandate for marriage.

It's quite possible your revered mother knows more than your beloved bride about raising kids, cooking, housecleaning, budgeting, calf-roping, parasailing, fly fishing, index averaging, and curing the common cold. None of that matters. Your brilliant mother may be a whiz at all those things and more. But you can't think that. And you shouldn't even believe that.

If your mom feels like she has been replaced, she has! Frankly, she should know better. One of a mom's key assignments is to prepare her children for marriage. Making a married son feel guilty about putting his wife first is a recipe for family disaster. Shame on her.

But back to your job as a husband. The expectation is clear. *Leave and cleave.* You know what *leave* means, but what about that other word? I turned to my trusty Merriam-Webster's Dictionary. That little-used word is actually a helpful description of what you and your bride need to do when it comes to the adventure of marriage:

> **Cleave:** verb: to adhere firmly and closely or loyally and unwaveringly.

Adhere. Firmly. Closely. Loyally. Unwaveringly. Son, do that and your mom will be very proud.

─────────────── **Takeaway** ───────────────

Don't allow in-law problems to get between you and your bride. Make sure the two of you are on the same page. Don't make enemies of the older generation. Honor them. But put your own family first.

"The family you came from isn't as important
as the family you're going to have."
Ring Lardner (1885–1933)

Wives Need Their Husbands...

To Buy Two Jars of Peanut Butter

O h the agony of marriage. So often couples bring opposite needs and expectations to their relationship. Drastic incompatibilities clash disastrously delivering devastating and divisive disharmony. What to do? What to do?

She likes coffee; he likes tea. She prefers action movies; he likes romantic comedies. She wants a beach vacation; he wants to take her to a four-star Manhattan hotel. He wants a spruce Christmas tree; she wants a Douglas fir. It's enough to make you stay single your entire life.

Yes, I know there are different viewpoints and requirements in most marriage relationships. Some might even seem to be deal breakers. But most are not. Most can and should be worked out. And that's the point.

Do you really argue over crunchy vs. creamy peanut butter? Buy two jars.

Is there debate about who makes the bed? It's the last person up.

Every January, do you clash over the setting on the thermostat? Invest in a cuddly comforter for whichever spouse gets the winter chills.

This is not rocket science, people. You married each other for better or worse. These little irritants may not be part of the "better," but they are not even in the vicinity of "worse." Unsnagging these minor snags just takes a smidge of common sense, a little extra effort, or a dash of compromise.

She flips out when you leave whiskers in the sink? Splash them away before you leave the bathroom.

You get ticked when she leaves the cap off the toothpaste? Is it really that big a deal?

You prefer Italian food and she prefers Mexican? You probably don't need to hire an attorney to negotiate the details of that peace accord.

Of course, the real topic of this chapter is not about dealing with differences. Differences are the spice of marriage. Your differences were the reason you got married in the first place. What you can't do, she can. And vice versa. You complete each other. The real purpose of this chapter is just to remind you to play nice. When it comes to silly little quirks and shortcomings, choose to be amused more than annoyed.

If you let them, there are plenty of things that can rob the joy from your day. Some of them you cannot control. But on all those teeny-weeny inconsequential issues, take the easy way out. Laugh them off. Do the easy fix. Find common ground.

On a serious note, there are some issues on which compromise isn't an option. In many marriages, one party might be required or requested to make a huge sacrifice and that shouldn't be taken lightly. Sometimes a husband or wife needs to set aside their own needs for the long-term benefit of the family. Situations arise: A mandatory cross-country move. A season caring for a loved one. Putting your spouse through school. Staying home to raise the kids. Months living apart due to military service or career responsibilities. Starting a new business. For the short term, these things will strain even the best marriages. Don't sugarcoat it. Acknowledge the sacrifice. Appreciate the partnership.

But if the biggest frustrations you have in your marriage are about TV remotes, wet towels, dirty dishes, lost car keys, scuff marks on the linoleum, "check engine" lights, thermostats, or peanut butter, then you'd better start counting your blessings. You've got a marriage made in heaven.

―――――――――――――― **Takeaway** ――――――――――――――

You know that one silly little issue she nags you about? Today, make it go away. You have that power.

"Keep your eyes wide open before marriage, half shut afterward."
Benjamin Franklin (1705–1790)

Wives Need Their Husbands…

To Install a Dead-Bolt Lock on the Bedroom Door

Guys, I don't think I have to tell you that we can be ready for romance at a moment's notice. That's how God made us. Being ready, willing, and able can be triggered by a TV commercial for auto parts or elevator music of a pretty bad song from the '80s. I confess that sometimes thoughts about having sex with my bride can be triggered unexpectedly in the middle of a busy workday by the mere mention of a particular city, car, artist, movie, style of shirt, candy bar, candle scent, restaurant, or season of the year. (The list is actually longer than that, but something distracted me from completing it.) I even remember one time a typo left a provocative word on my laptop and I lost focus for the rest of the afternoon, causing me to miss an editor's deadline. Blame love. (I may have blamed the delay on a problem with my computer, which wasn't a complete fib.)

While guys can be ready in a moment's notice, your bride can be derailed from sex just as quickly. You know the scenario. Maybe it's date night. Maybe it's a special occasion planned months in advance. Maybe it's a late-night rendezvous that you agreed to that morning and kept you motivated all day long. You're ready. She's just about ready. It's go time. But all that momentum and potential can be lost in an instant. Examples?

Your baby cries. Your third-grader pukes. Your high-schooler loses his cell phone and yells something about life being unfair. Your college student calls about her schizophrenic roommate. The furnace makes funny noises. The late local news has a story about a lost dog that looks like your wife's dog when she was little. Her mother calls to ask about Thanksgiving. Her mother doesn't call to ask about Thanksgiving. Or suddenly she's worried that one of the kids is going to come barging in at just the wrong time.

These are all potential deal breakers. None of them are your fault. Most of them you couldn't possibly predict or prevent.

On the other hand, maybe you should take some of the responsibility for the reason she is no longer "in the mood." Think back on the day. What did you do that you could have done differently? You mentioned the pot roast was a little dry. You said something about the new receptionist at work. You left the sprinkler on too long after she had just finished talking about the high water bill. You belched on your way to the bathroom. You left your socks on the floor. What are you, an idiot?

Actually, don't be too hard on yourself. It's all part of the game we call married life. Learn the rules and you've got a better chance of winning.

Veteran husbands have learned to be proactive when it comes to scheduling lovemaking and keeping potential distractions to a minimum. Tuck the little ones in yourself to make sure they are fast asleep. Do a sweep of the master bedroom to make sure nothing assaults the senses—extreme temperatures, dirty towels, peculiar smells, a stack of unpaid bills, or toothpaste in the sink. Offer a cup of herbal tea, glass of ice water, or some other nightcap to ensure your bride's comfort at the end of the day. Brush your teeth. Lock the bedroom door lest the rug rats invade.

Yes, we are at their mercy. In most marriages, men are the initiators and women are the final gatekeepers in this arena. And that's okay.

In a way, their sensitive nature and need to have everything "just right" prevents us from taking our brides for granted. We appreciate them all the more. When we do get the green light, we have learned to make the very best of it. And they appreciate our efforts all the more.

It's nice to be appreciated.

Takeaway

You married her because she was different than you. Don't be surprised if she's still different than you.

"Women need a reason to have sex. Men just need a place."
BILLY CRYSTAL (1947–)

Wives Need Their Husbands…

To Hit Bottom Together

The year is 1983. I've got two preschool boys at home. We're a month (or two) behind on our FHA mortgage. And I'm trying to make a living selling law books to corporate attorneys. I own three suits that are getting shabbier by the month, and my lone pair of black wingtips once belonged to my grandfather, who passed away five years earlier.

I am not a good salesman. It's not that I'm afraid of cold calls or lack initiative. I think I'm just too respectful of people's time and I don't want to be a pest. Clearly, the sales game is not for me. Something has to change.

Even in the midst of my job angst, life is not all bad. My young boys are healthy and smart. We're plugged in at church. The core values of who we are as a family are exactly right. But schlepping a 26-pound briefcase with law book samples around the Chicago Loop and coming up short on sales quotas again and again are taking their toll. For guys, job satisfaction ranks high on our priorities, and mine could not be any lower. My boyish charm and innate optimism are wearing thin. The world I once had been destined to conquer is beating me up and dragging me down. And Rita is well aware of it.

In this situation, couples cope in a variety of ways. Options include frequent screaming matches, denial and false optimism, running home to Mommy and Daddy, working double overtimes, or waiting to get fired and taking unemployment. I'm not sure if we chose our method of coping or it chose us, but for a year or so we stayed the course, found joy in small victories, and tried not to get further behind. Most of our mutual despondency remained unspoken. Until Rita spoke.

I was standing in the kitchen doorway. Her voice was quiet, not accusing. She said, "I don't have faith in you anymore."

Husbands, can you feel my pain? To be sure, this was not a physical assault or divorce papers being served. It wasn't an accusation of abuse, addiction, or adultery. It was simply a young wife and mother telling her husband exactly what he needed to hear. She was my committed partner in this adventure called life and she was also smart enough to put into words what I already knew. Standing in that doorway I experienced one of the worst and best moments of my life.

No, I didn't become a better salesman. That would have been impossible. But I did write those seven words on a three-by-five card and pushpin it on the wall above my desk: "I don't have faith in you anymore." I'm glad—and a little proud—to say I took it the right way. I stopped feeling sorry for myself. I hustled a little more. Reevaluated my gifts, passions, and career options. My wife and I intentionally spent more time talking about goals, life strategies, hopes, and dreams.

In the summer of 1984, I changed careers. I was offered an entry-level copywriter position at a small advertising agency on Michigan Avenue. It was a direct result of those hopes and dreams and goals we had talked about. When I told Rita the new job would actually reduce our income, she didn't hesitate. My young bride proved once again that she knew who I was and what I needed to hear. She said, "We'll make it work."

A quarter-century later, I still can't sell anything. But the mortgage is getting paid, my four sons have college degrees, my daughter is just starting college, and we haven't missed a meal. And Rita and I have one more little joke that gets sprinkled into our current conversations about goals, life strategies, hopes, and dreams. I'll say, "Do you have faith in me?" And she gets that twinkle in her eye and says, "For now."

Takeaway

When you hit bottom—and I hope you do—make sure your bride joins you in the darkness of the abyss. It will take both of you reaching, lifting, boosting, and supporting each other to crawl out into the sun.

"You may not realize it when it happens, but a kick in the teeth may be the best thing in the world for you."
Walt Disney (1901–1966)

Wives Need Their Husbands...

To Be Sane on Valentine's Day

D on't miss it. Don't go overboard. Find a nice middle ground. And for heaven's sake get all shopping and ordering out of the way a week before February 14.

I confess, more than once I have been part of the last-minute surge. The scene at the greeting-card rack is especially pathetic. You and a dozen other sorry-looking guys stand at the decimated and depleted supply of dog-eared cards, all knowing that you'll have to settle for leftovers. You'd be better off closing your eyes and just picking one. If you're fortunate to find a card that's not embarrassing, good luck finding an envelope to match.

Not that a fresh, full selection of cards is any better. Even when you shop for cards in January, most of the preprinted sentiments seem more like apologies than love notes.

"I know I don't say it enough...but I really do love you."

"I know I've been ignoring you recently...but I really do love you."

"This has been a cruddy year and I've been a total jerk...but I really do love you."

Who buys these cards? Maybe we should applaud when a husband realizes he falls a little short in his commitment to his marriage, but yikes. I hope those guys don't think Hallmark is going to make their subpar marriage relationship all peachy keen. If you found yourself drawn to (or buying) one of these "apology" cards, I hope you jotted a little bonus note on the inside. Something like, *Sweetheart, consider this my wake-up call. I am no longer going to take you for granted. I pledge to put your needs before my needs and I give you permission to hold me accountable.* Now that's a card worth saving.

Also, don't expect to walk into a florist at the last minute and be taken seriously. One year, I tried to place an order on February 12 and got laughed at.

Consider yourself lucky if you are able to find a pre-assembled bouquet that isn't dead or smashed. Grab it, throw your 60 bucks on the counter, and get out before some other poor schlub beats you to it.

Candy is a highly questionable gift for all kinds of reasons. Last year, our local Jewel Supermarket had two-for-one Fannie May Mint Meltaways as a Valentine's Day special. Honestly, two-for-one? What do they recommend a husband does with the second box? Save it for next year? Pig out in the parking lot? Give one to his wife and one to his girlfriend? (Not a possibility for you, I hope.) Maybe he should drive across town and deliver it to his mom. That would probably be the best choice.

In the same supermarket, I saw a dad following his two young sons, who were skipping toward the checkout. All three were holding Valentines for the same lucky lady. I liked that.

So that's lesson one. Order flowers early. Find a card early. And go easy on the chocolates.

Lesson two is about shopping for lingerie. While it's not a recommended anniversary gift (see chapter 37), under the right circumstances you do have permission to buy some nice, flattering, comfy jammies for Valentine's Day. Not too revealing or flamboyant, but maybe a little naughty. Just enough to let her know that you think of her as attractive, irresistible, and the love of your life. Sadly, I can no longer recommend a trip to Victoria's Secret. Recent commercials border on scandalous. And maybe I'm just getting older and out of touch, but the stores themselves seem to have gotten creepier and creepier over the last decade.

Lesson three is for you guys who make the rest of us look bad. Unless there's something special going on, save the romantic weekend escapes for another time of year. And don't be dropping a month's salary on some diamond tennis bracelet. Wives talk to each other, and husbands need to unite and keep Valentine gifts at a reasonable amount. Spend more than a hundred bucks or so and you're setting all your married buddies up for a deep freeze from their own wives that may last until summer.

And if there's a fourth lesson for Valentine's Day, it's this. Being thoughtful on February 14 doesn't let you off the hook the other 364 days of the year.

———————————— **Takeaway** ————————————

In the end, with all it stands for and all the opportunities it presents, maybe Valentine's Day is worth the hassle after all. Hey, any excuse for an extra smooch works for me.

> *"There are two kinds of people in the world:*
> *those who love chocolate, and communists."*
>
> LESLIE MOAK MURRAY

Wives Need Their Husbands…

To Laugh at Marriage

I love quotations. Send me an amusing or thought-provoking quote and I'll be your friend for life. Writing and researching this book, I perused hundreds of quotations on marriage. About two-thirds were unusable because they had a regretful negative view of marriage. I had promised myself—and my publisher and readers—that I would not berate husbands for being men. And I would not paint marriage as a terrible burden that we are forced to survive with gritted teeth and a broken spirit.

However, I found myself chuckling at quite a few of those "negative" quotes on marriage. Many of them had a point. Some were said with tongue in cheek. For many of them, you needed to consider the source. Playwrights, novelists, screenwriters, and comedians get paid for presenting life with a grain of truth and a twist of the knife. With that caveat, I share them with you.

> *I love being married. It's so great to find that one special
> person you want to annoy for the rest of your life.*
>
> —RITA RUDNER

> *Women marry men hoping they will change. Men marry women
> hoping they will not. So each is inevitably disappointed.*
>
> —ALBERT EINSTEIN

> *Never go to bed mad. Stay up and fight.*
>
> —PHYLLIS DILLER

> *I have learned that only two things are necessary to
> keep one's wife happy. First, let her think she's having
> her own way. And second, let her have it.*
>
> —LYNDON B. JOHNSON

*I never knew what real happiness was until I got
married. And by then it was too late.*

—MAX KAUFFMAN

*I'm an excellent housekeeper. Every time
I get a divorce, I keep the house.*

—ZSA ZSA GABOR

*The majority of husbands remind me of an
orangutan trying to play the violin.*

—HONORÉ DE BALZAC

*God made man, and then said, "I can do
better than that" and made woman.*

—ADELA ROGERS ST. JOHN

*The most happy marriage I can imagine to myself would
be the union of a deaf man to a blind woman.*

—SAMUEL TAYLOR COLERIDGE

*I never married because there was no need. I have three pets
at home which answer the same purpose as a husband. I have
a dog which growls every morning, a parrot which swears
all afternoon, and a cat that comes home late at night.*

—MARIE CORELLI

*Do you know what it means to come home at night to a woman
who'll give you a little love, a little affection, a little tenderness?
It means you're in the wrong house, that's what it means.*

—HENNY YOUNGMAN

*When a man steals your wife, there is no better
revenge than to let him keep her.*

—SACHA GUITRY

*When a man opens the car door for his wife,
it's either a new car or a new wife.*

—PRINCE PHILIP

The secret of a happy marriage remains a secret.

—HENNY YOUNGMAN

*Take care of him. And make him feel important.
And if you can do that, you'll have a happy and wonderful
marriage. Like two out of every ten couples.*

—NEIL SIMON

*Before marriage, a man declares that he would lay
down his life to serve you; after marriage, he won't
even lay down his newspaper to talk to you.*

—HELEN ROWLAND

*As to marriage or celibacy, let a man take which
course he will, he will be sure to repent.*

—SOCRATES

Marriage is the only war in which you sleep with the enemy.

—LA ROCHEFOUCAULD

*I don't think I'll get married again. I'll just find a
woman I don't like and give her a house.*

—LEWIS GRIZZARD

So there you have it. A cynical, jaundiced view of marriage. Do you buy into it? Do you get up every morning wondering what kind of argument or head-butting awaits you during the coming hours? Is that your expectation of marriage? Then maybe you deserve what you get.

If you believe the comedians, playwrights, media, and naysayers, marriage is either a prison or a battleground. But shifting those expectations or turning them upside down will go a long way toward growing a marriage that is made in heaven.

Still, don't leave this chapter without acknowledging that many a truth is said in jest. If you ever find yourself chuckling at a particular one-liner, comic strip, or sitcom joke that mocks the institution of marriage, it might be that you have uncovered one of the areas you need to work on with your bride.

So maybe this chapter wasn't a waste of time after all.

Takeaway

Spend enough time celebrating the good stuff in your marriage and you can laugh at the stuff that isn't quite worth celebrating.

*"You might not always get what you want,
but you always get what you expect."*

CHARLES SPURGEON (1834–1892)

Wives Need Their Husbands...

To Warehouse Memories Together

I f you haven't picked up on this point, I need to clarify something. Friend, I do not have all the answers. Seriously, if you picked up this book expecting to discover the exact 52 things that every wife needs from her husband, then I apologize. Any man who claims he does have all the keys to wedded bliss is either a liar or a lunatic. Or has never been married.

Almost by accident, you may find some truths and hard-earned lessons sprinkled in these pages. But like all of us, I am still learning. Thankfully, I have had a couple of pretty good teachers. As of this writing, my mom and dad are still a role model for me after more than 60 years of marriage. One of the greatest things they did for our family is create a home worth coming home to. That was never clearer than last fall when they moved out of the house in which they had lived for 35 years.

For most of the summer, their four kids (Mary Kay, Mark, Sue, and I), our spouses, and several of our kids helped sort necessities and pack cardboard boxes to take with them to their new place. It was an emotional time. Not painful, but difficult. And wonderful. And rewarding.

Digging through unintentional family archives opens the heart and mind to an onslaught of memories. I remember thinking, *This stuff could fill a museum. A museum that only Payleitners would want to visit.*

What were the most glorious finds of this suburban archaeological dig?

- My mom's classic black Singer sewing machine on which she created entire summer wardrobes for my little sister "Susie."

- A photo of my dad at age 34 in his office as an elementary-school principal. A black dial phone, a fountain pen, and a few file folders sit on his desk. His black suit and skinny artsy tie are awesome. Hipsters today would kill for that outfit.

- The hand-tooled iron machine part crafted by my mom in 1942 in high-school shop class. The girls were being trained to man the factories because the boys were being trained to stop the Nazis and the Japanese.

- Baseballs and photos actually touched and autographed by potentially awesome Chicago Cubs players from bygone years. Most of their signatures are indecipherable.

- A ceramic mug adorned with a grandfatherly face that once held nickels for our milk money.

- Faded plastic flowers.

- Six cans of WD-40. They must have been on sale.

- A hundred VHS tapes. (Including a two-tape set of country line-dancing videocassettes. Yikes!)

- A cloth bag of perhaps 40 JFK half-dollars.

- The imitation leather–bound *Encyclopedia Britannica* set, including the "M" volume with wrinkled pages and swollen binding. In 1967 I took it to school to work on my report on minks (the animal). I left that particular volume in the backyard overnight in the rain. I don't think I ever confessed to that misdeed. Until now.

- The fireplace bellows that was used more often to puff air into the faces of siblings than to fan a fire. (Also used to torture the dog and cats.)

- The six or eight sets of kitchen knives earned by my parents for opening a new charge account or listening to a sales pitch.

- Nana's fancy blue candy dish. Wrapped in 20-year-old newsprint. And accidentally shattered.

- The lime-green seat cushion/life preserver on which my grandfather Fritz Payleitner perched for hours and hours to catch perch, crappies, and northern pike. At Pine Lake. He's been gone 32 years, but I can still picture him proudly holding up a stringer of his day's catch.

- And of course, the tools in my dad's workshop. Seven hammers. Twelve pliers. Forty screwdrivers. Two million assorted bolts, screws, and nails.

My folks are actually doing well. I will not spell out their ailments here. We four kids are doing just fine. Our spouses too. The eleven grandkids are phenomenal. Plus, my parents even have a couple of great-grandchildren.

All in all, we're a fairly functional family. We get along. We laugh a lot. I look forward to our times together. We're just about always on the same wavelength when it comes to life decisions large and small. When we're not, we sort out disagreements with candor, respect, and love.

I know that it's the family—not the house—that makes a home. Still, I won't soon forget the summer spent boxing up stuff and preparing for a modest estate sale and my mom and dad's two-mile move to a senior living apartment.

I wonder, when the packing tape seals a cardboard box, what happens to the memories? Some, I fear, are lost. But the memories that matter settle comfortably in the crevices between yesterday and tomorrow.

If you so desire, they can be retrieved with just a little effort.

Takeaway

You may think your most daunting task is making a home for your children, but really your truest priority is making memories.

"God gave us memories that we might have roses in December."

J.M. BARRIE (1860–1937)

Wives Need Their Husbands...

To Try This Experiment

For the next three days, pick six fights with your wife. That's a total of eighteen arguments. Here are eighteen suggested squabble starters. Although I'm sure you can come up with several unique to your own marriage relationship.

1. "I'm thinking you wear a little too much makeup."

2. "I'm thinking you need to wear a little more makeup."

3. "Didn't we just have this same thing for dinner last week?"

4. "Let me know when your 'creative cooking' kick is over."

5. "Did you see the new women's fitness center that just opened down the street?"

6. "You know, these mugs you bought don't fit in the dishwasher."

7. "Two hundred channels and this is what you're watching?"

8. "Did you see what your son did? Why do you let him get away with that?"

9. "Actually, I'm not really hungry. I had a late lunch. I had to go over a proposal with Amber from marketing."

10. "Did you really need another pair of shoes?"

11. "Your way is not really wrong, but my mom used to do it this way."

12. "How much was that haircut again?"

13. "You always…"

14. "You never..."

15. "So which is it tonight? Are you too tired, too distracted, or too crampy, or do you just have your regular ten o'clock headache?"

16. "You never, ever put the top back on the toothpaste. It's really unbelievable."

17. "What happened to your skinny jeans?"

18. "How old was your mother when she started going gray?"

A word of caution before you begin this experiment. *Don't.* Do not go there. Do not repeat any of these malicious statements. Because your wife actually cares about what you think, she is too easy and too vulnerable a target. And life is too precious.

Reading through the above list, I'm guessing you easily came up with your own versions of squabble starters, didn't you? And that's the point. These kind of troublemaking thoughts creep through our minds on a daily basis. You could quite easily start a petty argument during every conversation you ever have with your wife. And that petty argument could easily escalate into a barrage of words and accusations that are not even true. And that barrage of words and accusations could easily escalate into several days of silence and cold stares. And those days of silence and cold stares could easily escalate into threats of ripping the family apart. *So true*

Am I exaggerating? In some cases, that's exactly how a marriage falls apart. It's not one big thing. It's an exhausting and divisive avalanche of little, hurtful, inconsiderate words and actions.

So again—don't go there.

When those snappy little retorts, complaints, or innuendos pop into your head, leave them there. Just say no. Don't allow any of those potential fighting words to reach your tongue. Disaster averted.

Now here's the real experiment. For the next three days, say six nice things to your wife each day. I'll let you make your own list.

Let me know how it goes.

Takeaway

Before you say it, you know you shouldn't say it—so why do you still say it? Instead, don't say it, and before long you may not even think it.

"Words from the mouth of a wise man are gracious,
while the lips of a fool consume him."

ECCLESIASTES 10:12 NASB

Wives Need Their Husbands...

To Read the Verses that Come Before and After Ephesians 5:22

Y ou gotta love Ephesians 5:22: "Wives, submit to your husbands as to the Lord."

You also have to admit that this verse has caused quite a bit of controversy in and outside of the church in recent years. A feminist quotes this verse to prove that the Bible is archaic and irrelevant. A biblically illiterate Neanderthal quotes this verse to keep his wife in a subservient role, insisting her opinion has no value and her contribution to the household is limited to cooking, cleaning, and keeping herself available for his sexual whims.

Yikes. In my house—and I hope in yours—the Bible is ubiquitously relevant and I definitely need my wife to be something other than an unpaid servant and prostitute.

Upon further examination, you'll discover that this verse and the surrounding passage are all about empowerment for every member of the family. To put any controversy behind us once and for all, let's take a look at Ephesians 5:22 in context.

First off, let's begin with the nine words immediately preceding that verse. Ephesians 5:21 says quite plainly, "Submit to one another out of reverence for Christ." That's pretty clear. The apostle Paul was writing to believers in the church at Ephesus and all believers everywhere. He expected all of us to have the heart of a servant and put the needs of others first.

Then after introducing the concept of submitting to one another, Paul gives three examples of how that works in real life for wives, husbands, and kids. Because strong families are the building blocks of a society, that's where he started. And because men, women, and children have different needs, Paul explains how to honor and affirm each of them differently. Men need to lead. Women need to feel cherished. Children need instruction. Read it for yourself.

> Wives, submit to your husbands as to the Lord. For the husband is the head of the wife as Christ is the head of the church, his body, of which he is the Savior (Ephesians 5:22-23).

> Husbands, love your wives, just as Christ loved the church and gave himself up for her…In this same way, husbands ought to love their wives as their own bodies. He who loves his wife loves himself (5:25,28).

> Children, obey your parents in the Lord, for this is right (6:1).

Husbands, did you hear your marching orders? Your wife needs you to take a leadership role. But you need to lead with love. Sacrificial love. Just like Christ gave his life for us, we need to willingly give our lives for our brides.

Now some of you are thinking, *I can do that. I would certainly rescue my wife from a rampaging wildebeest or leap in front of an assassin's bullet for her. That might even be way cool.* Sorry, guys…if only it were that easy. Since those action-packed scenarios are probably not going to happen, you need to think in terms of sacrificing something much more mundane. Loving your wife sacrificially means putting her well-being before your own when it comes to your time, energy, resources, creativity, and even your will. That's right. You lead…for her sake.

If she's unhappy, suffering, discouraged, ignored, or feeling unloved, there's a problem. Look again at Ephesians 5:21: "Submit to one another out of reverence for Christ."

Some theologians call it "mutual submission." Others don't like that term, but it's a pretty accurate paraphrase of how the Bible describes a successful marriage. He sacrifices. She submits. Both are looking for the best in each other and looking out for each other.

For the record, no place in the Bible does it tell women specifically to "obey your husbands." "Love, honor, and obey" were once part of the wedding vows, but you won't hear that at many of today's wedding ceremonies.

The word "obey" is saved for the kids. This is good news. It's still okay for mom and dad to expect obedience from the next generation.

So next time you hear someone misquote Ephesians 5:22, you are now equipped to get in his or her face and say, "Pal, I think you're taking that verse out of context. Have you even read that complete passage of the Bible? Do you know that it's really all about giving wives and husbands equal authority when it comes to decision-making?"

Okay. Now that I've stirred up that hornet's nest, I'd love to hear from you. That's jaypayleitner.com. Looking forward to it.

Takeaway

Just about every time some knucklehead starts yammering about the dangers or unfairness of a particular Bible verse, you can bet that they have not read the entire passage.

"There is nothing more admirable than two people who see eye-to-eye keeping house as man and wife, confounding their enemies, and delighting their friends."

HOMER (NINTH CENTURY BC)

Wives Need Their Husbands...

To Say "I'm Really Sorry" Like You Really Mean It

This is an easy chapter to write. Because I'm very good at asking forgiveness. Maybe that's because I've had a lot of practice.

I've apologized to umpires when I yell too much at ball games. I've apologized to all five of my kids when work deadlines are nipping at my heels and I snap at them after they inadvertently derail my train of thought. I apologize for taking corners too fast and laying down Scrabble tiles too slowly. I apologize for sometimes serving lukewarm pop and lukewarm pizza.

And yes, I apologize to my bride on a regular basis. I apologize for being wrong—even when I'm not 100 percent sure that I am.

Sometimes I think I may apologize too much. But in truth my infractions most definitely outnumber my confessions. I recall some insight I heard from a friend who happens to be a cop. I was complaining to him about a ticket I received in another city for going a paltry 8 miles an hour over the speed limit. His reply was, "Yeah, that might seem unfair. But just think about all the times you were going 15 over the limit and didn't get pulled over."

We mess up. We sin. That's our human condition.

So here's my stand on asking forgiveness. As men and leaders of our family we should take a position of responsibility. Which means if good things happen, we can take some of the credit. But when bad things happen, we need to take most of the blame.

Asking forgiveness is a great tool for keeping the peace. It's a great way to say, "Please give me another chance." Asking forgiveness and giving forgiveness is what Christians do. Because we have a great teacher: Jesus himself.

In the Lord's Prayer, Jesus reminds us that we need to regularly ask God for forgiveness and forgive others who have done us wrong (see Matthew 6:12).

In Proverbs, we're told that when we admit our screw-ups we'll prosper and maybe even get a little mercy and sympathy: "He who conceals his transgressions will not prosper, but he who confesses and forsakes them will find compassion" (Proverbs 28:13 NASB).

The Bible also confirms that admitting our sins and asking forgiveness makes us right before God. That's the best and only way we have to clean up our act. "If we confess our sins, he is faithful and just and will forgive us our sins and purify us from all unrighteousness" (1 John 1:9).

In marriage, being quick to forgive and quick to ask forgiveness makes life way easier. Show of hands—how many of you have messed up, stubbornly refused to repent, and suffered two or three weeks of the cold shoulder from your wife? Wouldn't it have been a lot easier on you (and your bride) if you had delivered a sincere, authentic, and timely apology?

Why are we so pig-headed about this?

Take it from someone who knows—that's me—take responsibility early and often. If the oatmeal is cold or the toilet seat is up, say "I'm sorry." If you drank the last Diet Coke or allowed the water softener to run out of salt, say "My bad." Those are relatively minor infractions. But a quick apology is good practice for when you *really* self-destruct.

Once a year, when you say something terribly stupid, forget something terribly important, or do something terribly disgraceful, you'll be much better equipped to do what you need to do.

On those occasions, you may want to take the following steps to prepare and deliver an apology to your worthy bride, whom you love more than life itself. Find a quiet place. Do several minutes or more of soul-searching. Consider what you said or did from her perspective. Take responsibility. Decide what kind of promise or restitution needs to be made. Can you legitimately promise to never say that or do it again? Is there a way to fix the problem or take away some of the pain or hurt feelings? Would a gift or some giant gesture help?

Then go to her. The time and place is important. This may take a while and it may not be pretty. You probably don't need to rehash a detailed account of what you did. But you do need to acknowledge the damage you've done. Express remorse. Ask forgiveness. The words "I'm so sorry" still work well. Make a promise. Suggest some form of sacrificial reparation. The goal is a kiss. A hug might be all you get. Take it.

There's an undeniable spiritual dimension to forgiveness. We need to be eager participants when we do wrong and are wronged. I invite you to meditate on these words Paul wrote from inside a prison cell to the Colossian church:

> Clothe yourselves with compassion, kindness, humility, gentleness and patience. Bear with each other and forgive whatever grievances you may have against one another. Forgive as the Lord forgave you. And over all these virtues put on love, which binds them all together in perfect unity (Colossians 3:12-14).

Takeaway

Asking forgiveness is not a sign of weakness—it's proof that you are strong enough to take responsibility for who you are and what you do—the good and the bad.

"Forgiveness does not change the past,
but it does enlarge the future."
PAUL BOESE (1668–1738)

Wives Need Their Husbands…

To Hug Julie Bryant Without Guilt

J ulie Bryant is strawberry-blonde, cute, and several years younger than me. She and I spent ten days together in a foreign country. Next time I see Julie I expect to give her a big hug. And that's absolutely okay with my wife, Rita. (At least I think it is.)

Some additional information might be helpful here. Julie and I were part of Operation Carelift 1996 with the Josh McDowell Ministry. As part of the media team, our primary responsibility was to gather stories from Russian pastors, volunteers, and ministry staff to tell back home in radio programs and other media. In addition, we got to stretch our personal ministry muscles in schools, hospitals, and orphanages in and around Moscow. For those ten days we were pretty important to each other, and together we did some work that made a real difference in the lives of real people. That kind of experience stays with you for a long time. And I recommend it.

Julie and I literally have not seen each other in more than a decade, and she has since gotten married. Every Christmas, I send her a batch of angel ornaments to distribute among select co-workers at the agency in Seattle where she still works for nonprofit organizations. A ten-minute phone call catches us up.

Here's the point. For me, Julie is the exception to the rule. In general, I should not be hugging other women. And neither should you. The reasons are many.

It may send the wrong signal to the woman being hugged. It may offend her husband. It may give your own wife something to worry about. It may trigger your own imagination regarding longer hugs and more. It may just be creepy.

Now I could get into specific kinds of hugs. We could talk about side hugs, pat-on-the-back hugs, and leaning hugs where there is very little body contact. I could pull out a stopwatch and suggest that a 1.5-second hug is okay, but a 2-second hug is not. I could suggest that husbands all make a list of six women that you are allowed to hug and even create a little laminated card for your wallet. But a list of concrete hugging rules is probably not the best answer.

Instead of making rules, let's all just pledge to be aware. When a friend's father dies, give her a hug at the funeral. When your sister-in-law gets her master's degree, give her a big congratulatory hug. When an old comrade from a mission trip comes to town, give her a hug and share some memories.

However, if you find yourself hugging too much and too long, consider backing off. If your own wife is not in the room, be extra careful. If you find yourself keeping secrets from your wife or conveniently not mentioning women you happen to meet, that's a bright-red warning flag. Practice full disclosure after any and every hug. Example: "Sweetheart, you'll never guess who I saw at Starbucks this morning. Colleen from our old couples group! I gave her a big hug. She says hi. And I caught her up on all the news about our family."

So gentlemen, take this as a cautionary tale. I'm not accusing you of cheating on your wife or even any impure thoughts. I'm just saying. And I think you know what I mean.

And Julie, next time we meet, maybe I'll just shake your hand. I hear your husband is a pretty big guy.

Takeaway

Protect your marriage.

> *"Quit kidding yourself. Understand the tremendous capacity of every human being to deceive him or herself when not connected to God. Know that, once you start making excuses for wrong behavior, each excuse will sound more plausible, and you will sink deeper and deeper into sin and ruin. Admit that you can't trust your own self apart from God, and decide to stay close to Him."*
>
> Jerry Jenkins (1949–), from his book
> *Hedges: Loving Your Marriage Enough to Protect It*

Wives Need Their Husbands…

To Ask "Is This Okay?"

I t took me 25 years to learn this.

Rita and I are getting ready to go someplace where we will be in the presence of other people. A party, a restaurant, church, a wedding, a funeral. Some place that requires me to look a little sharper than my typical home-office schlub look.

I'm not a big clothes guy. I'm glad to be an author, which allows me to stay at home in comfy jeans and a raggedy long-sleeve T for days on end. With the new technology, I even do most of my radio-production work at home, sending and receiving audio files through the Internet.

Anyway. I totally understand that sometimes wrinkles, frayed collars, styles from the 1980s, and clashing colors and patterns are bad. While complementary colors, seasonal awareness, polished shoes, and general tidiness are good. I'm not a total dweeb. But I respect my wife's opinion and want her to not be embarrassed by me.

Here's the big lesson I learned, and now I pass it on to you.

I used to stand in front of my closet and get mad at my wife because I knew when I finally came down the stairs she would find something wrong with what I was wearing. I would say, "Ready to go?" and she would find fault, just as I knew she would. *"How old is that shirt?" "If you're going to wear those pants, I need to iron them." "That tie is too wide." "Those socks? Really?"*

Of course, she means well. She married a handsome guy and doesn't want anyone at the event to think that she isn't taking care of her man. Besides, her tone isn't mocking, she's just trying to get it right.

The problem was that I was wasting precious energy attempting to figure out what she was going to say before she even said it. That is not a good place to be. So one day, instead of getting angry, I just gave up. I threw on what I thought was a reasonable outfit—nice jeans, oxford shirt, tweedy jacket— and trudged down the stairs.

Instead of saying, "Ready to go?" I said, "Is this okay?"

Brilliant! Suddenly, I had given her permission to judge. Permission to make an adjustment. Permission to second-guess me in this one area of life in which I was not an overachiever.

Strangely enough, on that particular day there were no wardrobe malfunctions. She said, "I think button one more button," and that was it. That day, I had struck fashion gold and learned a new trick for maintaining marital accord.

Since then, prepping for social gatherings has been a piece of cake. After asking, "Is this okay?" I have submitted to such formidable tasks as changing a shirt, putting on a tie, and standing by the ironing board in my boxers while Rita pressed my pants. None of which were a problem. After all, I had asked her opinion. When she gave it to me, she was actually following my instructions.

The benefits of my new discovery are many. There's never a fight about what I'm wearing. Less time digging in my closet. I look presentable. And we're making better use of each other's gifts. She's better than me at fashion. I'm better than her at modeling men's clothes. (Although she looks good in my shirts, but that's another story.)

A couple things to remember. First, when you say, "Is this okay?" use a tone that's matter-of-fact. Don't sneer it. Don't roll your eyes. The goal is to get a quick honest assessment, and if she suggests a change—minor or otherwise—just do it.

Second, if you give your wife permission to make a negative comment, it's not a negative comment at all. It may sound like one, but really it's an opinion you requested. Keep that in mind.

Like so many great ideas for husbands, this one has several parallel applications. "Is this okay?" or "What do you think?" can be used when picking a restaurant, a movie, vacation destination, or any number of decisions that need to be made.

Of course, not every choice should be thrown up for discussion. The longer you've been married, the more likely you are to know each other's preferences. Some choices like china patterns and drapes are better left totally to your bride. Which leaves you with complete executive authority over lawn fertilizer and driveway sealer.

Gentlemen, asking your bride's opinion early is always better than having her second-guess you after the decision has been made. Insisting on her input helps you maintain the illusion that you are in control.

Takeaway

The great benefit of sharing and listening to each other's opinions on the small stuff is that you're well-rehearsed when it comes to the big stuff.

"If I want your opinion, I'll give it to you."
SAMUEL GOLDWYN (1879–1974)

Wives Need Their Husbands...

To Be the Pastor of Your Home

Generations ago, the boundaries were clear. He was the breadwinner. She was the homemaker.

For better and worse, those boundaries are not quite so clear anymore. Both sides have taken on and given up responsibilities that have blurred gender roles. The result is that many husbands and wives have gotten to explore some talents and abilities that previously may have gone untapped. Surely, this has led to a new shared appreciation and respect for each other's contributions to the home. It's even possible that recent marriages have a fresh sense of cooperation, communication, and partnership. But what have we lost?

If both spouses are expected to do *all* things, then *some* things are going to get overlooked. Important things. Like spiritual leadership.

Before you start to panic because you think this is going to turn into a lecture, let me assure you that the idea of being a pastor in your own home is not as complicated as it sounds.

The simple formula is this: Be the best Christian you can be. Let your family see that effort. And then help them do the same.

Examples?

Pray. Let your wife and kids see and hear you pray. Encourage them to pray.

Seek forgiveness when you mess up. Let your family see and hear you seek forgiveness when you mess up. Encourage them to seek forgiveness when they mess up.

Give a sacrificial chunk of your income to the church and other Christ-honoring causes. Let your family see you do that. Challenge them to tithe as well.

Want more examples?

Read the Bible. Sing praise songs. Volunteer. Honor your mother and father. Don't curse. Tell the truth. Feed the hungry. Meet regularly in a small-group community for Bible study. Seek wise Christian counsel when you face a tough challenge. Keep your pride in check. Flee sexual immorality. Tell others about Jesus.

Let your family see you do those things. Encourage them to do the same. It's really an age-old, proven method for leadership.

Do. Model. Teach.

It's not complicated. It's also not easy. But like so many aspects of a surrendered, Christ-honoring life, the desire and struggle to do the right thing is pleasing to God.

Takeaway

Seek God's will. Let your family see you seeking God's will. Help them seek God's will.

"Believe in the Lord Jesus, and you will be saved—you and your household."

Acts 16:31

Wives Need Their Husbands...

To Co-Sponsor the Upcoming Empty Nest

F ast-forward in your mind a few years. Maybe a few decades. If you've had kids, they've moved out and onward. You're no longer building a career. You've settled into a profession that matches your gifts and—despite some ups and downs—you've learned how to be comfortable with your income and position. Or maybe you're officially retired.

Your knees creak, but it doesn't slow you down. Your savings could be more, but you're doing okay. You've checked off quite a few items on your bucket list, but you also realize some earthly goals and dreams may go unfulfilled. For the most part, it's all good.

How did you get here? Let's review.

The years of discovery. After the honeymoon, all kinds of habits, quirks, shortcomings, and wonderful surprises come to light for both you and your bride. Adjustments are made. Two become one.

> "Haven't you read the Scriptures?" Jesus replied. "They record that from the beginning 'God made them male and female.' And he said, 'This explains why a man leaves his father and mother and is joined to his wife, and the two are united into one'" (Matthew 19:4-5 NLT).

The years of blurred activity. Especially if you have multiple kids, it's stunning how many activities fill your weekly calendar. Your busyness might seem like a distraction from some bigger purpose, but don't beat yourself up. You're doing what you need to do. You're making priceless memories. And God's truth can be presented and applied to your family in the course of the busiest day.

> Love the LORD your God with all your heart and with all your soul and with all your strength. These commandments that I give you today are to be upon your hearts. Impress them on your children. Talk about them when you sit at home and when you walk along the road, when you lie down and when you get up (Deuteronomy 6:5-7).

The years of productivity. Like a well-oiled machine, you begin to discover your grownup gifts and abilities. You set aside some youthful dreams but replace them with projects and passions at which you excel and which actually contribute to the greater good. God's bigger picture for your life comes into focus.

> God is working in you, giving you the desire and the power to do what pleases him (Philippians 2:13 NLT).

The years of desperation. In our fallen world, bad stuff happens. Illness. Loss. Conflict. Trials. In those desperate seasons, some husbands and wives can allow struggles to drive a wedge between them. A better choice would be for those couples to seek God's face together and find a new maturity and appreciation for each other. Desperate times also give us a chance to discover a new awareness of God's comfort and provision.

> Consider it pure joy, my brothers and sisters, whenever you face trials of many kinds, because you know that the testing of your faith produces perseverance. Let perseverance finish its work so that you may be mature and complete, not lacking anything (James 1:2-4).

The years of appreciation. After (and sometimes between) periods of discovery, blurred activity, productivity, and desperation, you will be able to look back and see God at work. It's an astonishing view. His faithfulness is guaranteed. No matter how many times you've heard it, it's still humbling and comforting to realize he's big enough and strong enough to handle all your needs, doubts, frustrations, arrogance, and fears.

> As the heavens are higher than the earth, so are my ways higher
> than your ways and my thoughts than your thoughts (Isaiah 55:9).

The longer you walk with God, the more you get small glimpses of heaven and how all things work toward God's ultimate purpose for your life.

The years mentioned above are not really years at all, but periods of time—both long and short. Days or decades. They are also not sequential, and you'll find yourself moving in and out of these periods as events unfold and family members come and go.

The secret to surviving these tumultuous time spans? One, know that God can give purpose to your life. Two, trust that seasons change. Three, don't go it alone.

> Live happily with the woman you love through all the meaning-
> less days of life that God has given you under the sun. The wife
> God gives you is your reward for all your earthly toil (Ecclesias-
> tes 9:9 NLT).

Suddenly that empty nest you were so worried about becomes filled with memories, shared accomplishments, re-aligned priorities, soul-satisfying rewards, and a new sense of purpose.

Takeaway

Navigating through the tumultuous seasons of life leads a husband and wife to a depth of love and respect that mere newlyweds could not possibly understand.

> *"Grow old along with me. The best is yet to be,*
> *the last of life for which the first was made."*
> ROBERT BROWNING (1812–1889)

Wives Need Their Husbands...

To Not Take Financial Advice from Me

I f you are browsing, buy this book. If you own it, buy a few more for other men you know. I am pretty much counting on you to fund my retirement fund.

That's my way of saying that I am not very good at financial planning. My rainy-day savings have either washed away or dried up. My 401-K is not okay. And I certainly cannot count on my employer for any kind of substantial pension plan, because I'm self-employed.

On the math portion of the SAT and ACT, I scored in the top 1 percent. Really, I did. But having a mathematical mind does not necessarily translate to financial savvy. I am very, very grateful that Rita does the bill-paying. Early in our marriage I took it over for a few months, and I'm pretty sure we're still paying for my inept checkbook-balancing skills.

All that to say, between the two of you, I encourage you and your bride to come up with a wise financial plan and stick to it.

Since I am no expert, that's where this chapter should probably end. But let me take a stab at offering you a list of warnings and lessons, some of which I learned the hard way.

- If you change jobs, don't spend any money you may have accrued to your retirement plan. You will be tempted to spend it, but roll it over.

- If your place of employment offers some kind of automatic payroll-saving deduction, choose the maximum amount. Especially if they offer matching funds.

- If you haven't yet, start some investment with your very next pay-check. Even if it's just 20 bucks. You may think the money manager or investment counselor is going to laugh at a measly amount, but they won't. Everyone starts small.

- Buy slightly used cars and pay cash if at all possible. (Also, find a good mechanic you can trust.)

- The only thing you should really borrow money for is a house. Everything else you should only buy if you have the money in hand.

- Get a 15-year mortgage.

- Splurge rarely. Be frugal in spending 95 percent of the time, so that when you splurge, it's special! If you go out for steak and lobster every week, it loses its deliciousness.

- It's okay to use credit cards for convenience, but pay them off every month. I repeat. Pay them off every month.

- Never, ever be late with a credit-card payment. They will jack your interest rate up to 20, 25, even close to 30 percent.

- Do that tithing thing. It all belongs to God anyway. So instead of thinking that you're giving him 10 percent, realize that God is generously letting you keep 90 percent.

Did I mention that many of the above principles were learned the hard way? Believe it or not, some I am still not doing.

Clearly, I am no Larry Burkett, Ron Blue, or Dave Ramsey. Over the years, those gentlemen have applied biblical principles to money management and helped millions of people overcome debt and find a new level of contentment with money and retirement. You would do well to avail yourself of their resources and programs.

The best plan is to have a plan. Gentlemen, if this is an area in which you are not an expert, swallow your pride and get some wise counsel. Your church very likely offers some help in this area. Maybe your bride is a financial whiz.

You don't have to tackle this important area of life alone. Like so many things that have to get done, sometimes it's better for someone else to do it. But if you just let your financial health slide, it's going to come back and bite you real hard.

Trust me. And thanks for buying this book and contributing to the Jay and Rita Payleitner retirement fund.

Takeaway

When it comes to money, I wish I knew then what I know now.

"A successful man is one who makes more money than his wife can spend. A successful woman is one who can find such a man."
LANA TURNER (1921–1995)

Wives Need Their Husbands...

To Only Have Eyes for Her

When you got married you promised to remain sexually faithful to your wife, right? That's still a worthy goal, right? Well, good news. I can help you with that.

If you're an adult male, you cannot deny the power of a flash of flesh to draw your attention. A too-short skirt. A hint of cleavage. It's really an incredible force of nature. Most women understand that a revealing outfit brings a certain amount of attraction from males, but they have no idea how much power they really have. Every man reading this is well aware of that power. Whether it's an inadvertent half-second glimpse at a Victoria's Secret ad or four hours drinking and drooling at a rundown strip club, the images entrap us. Those examples are extreme, but they're both examples of a creepy little four-letter word: *lust.*

You've already committed to making sure there is no sex outside of marriage, but what about lust? Did you know that lust and adultery are virtually the same issue? Jesus made the connection in Matthew 5:28: "I tell you that anyone who looks at a woman lustfully has already committed adultery with her in his heart."

That idea is a bit of a stunner. Quite a few guys operate under the rules, "It's okay to look, but don't touch." But that won't work. Jesus says you can't touch and you can't look either. Unless you're looking at or touching your wife.

Which brings me to a slightly controversial recommendation. This idea actually takes the creepiness out of the word *lust.* It's simple: Lust after your wife. And only your wife. Make her the object of your visual fantasies. Make her your standard of the perfect woman. Refuse to accept the world's manufactured version of counterfeit beauty based on airbrushed photos, surgical body and face sculpting, and hours with a cosmetologist. Look at your bride as if you were on a desert island. If it were just the two of you, she would be your ultimate prize. Which is convenient because when you became husband and wife she was saying that's exactly what she wants to be—the one woman perfect for you!

So instead of struggling to say no to the beauty of the female form, say yes. Appreciate your bride's every curve and angle. Her smile. Her eyes. The hidden beauty of what she reveals to you alone.

This concept is especially gratifying to the 99 percent of women who hate what they see in a mirror. For a woman, if her husband sincerely sees her as beautiful, that's all she really needs to know.

By the way, the Bible backs up the idea of a godly man looking at his wife with extreme desire. Ezekiel's wife is called the "desire of his eyes" (Ezekiel 24:16 NASB). Solomon told his wife, "How beautiful and how delightful you are, my love, with all your charms! Your stature is like a palm tree, and your breasts are like its clusters. I said, 'I will climb the palm tree, I will take hold of its fruit stalks'" (Song of Solomon 7:6-8 NASB).

I happen to have a beautiful wife. I'm guessing you do too. But that no longer needs to be a factor in our minds, because there is no longer anyone to compare them to. We can choose to remove any and all competition. By default, your bride is the most beautiful woman in your world.

Today, start to act like that. Start to believe it. And if you dare, tell her she is the most beautiful creature on the planet.

Author's note: If the idea of "lusting" after your wife seems vulgar, please re-read the above chapter and replace that word with the concept of "visually longing" for your wife. Make sense?

Takeaway

Your wife is as beautiful as you see her.

"Love looks not with the eyes, but with the mind;
and therefore is winged Cupid painted blind."

William Shakespeare (1564–1616)
from *A Midsummer Night's Dream*

Wives Need Their Husbands...

To Initiate Closure to Arguments

ave you noticed that guys apologize much more often than gals? I'm not
sure why that is, but it has to be one of three reasons.

Perhaps we mess up more. Which should not be surprising because guys
take more risks. We may not always consider every possible pitfall when we
begin a journey or a conversation. It's our conquering spirit. When something needs to be done, we do it. When something needs to be said, we say it.
When something needs to be joked about, we joke about it. When something
needs to be yelled at a referee, we yell it. It's all preprogrammed into the male
genetic code and therefore it is not really our fault even when it is our fault.
Still, when presented with the burden of evidence, any judge would find us
guilty, so in the end we're the ones saying, "I'm sorry."

Maybe we're just more magnanimous.* When there is some undetermined
factor bringing disharmony to a relationship, we rise above it. It couldn't possibly be our fault, but our nobility and generous spirit prompts us to take the
blame. This is the same instinct that leads a soldier in a foxhole to jump on
a grenade. (A chick would never do that.) We take one for the team. Even if
we are not guilty, we take the punch and roll with it. In short, I'm not admitting that we mess up more. We just know that someone has to apologize and,
rather than pussyfoot around, we take charge of the situation. We're men.
We're noble creatures. We man up.

The third reason husbands apologize more might be that we just can't hold
out as long as our wives. Let's say the two of you are in a little marital spat. The

---

* Magnanimous: adjective, defined as 1) showing or suggesting a lofty and courageous spirit, 2) showing
  or suggesting nobility of feeling and generosity of mind.

reason doesn't matter. Toilet seat up. Overdrawn bank account. Underwear on the floor. TV show didn't get recorded. Someone forgot to use a coaster. Someone forgot an anniversary. Someone said something unpleasant about their mother-in-law. Whatever. There's a little tension in the air. Unpleasant words are exchanged. For a few days, no words are exchanged. Kisses and other benefits of marriage are definitely out of the question.

As the pages in the calendar turn, it becomes quite obvious that your wife is in no hurry to put this spat in the past. A couple more days and you realize that the term *weaker sex* has nothing to do with perseverance. You are the one feeling weak. You desperately want things to go back to normal, and she seems to have created an entire new standard for normal. And it's not pleasant. At this point, you have little choice but to apologize. You may not even remember exactly what you did wrong. Like a prisoner waiting for trial, you may have already paid for your misdeeds with time served in the doghouse. Even if you are totally innocent, your wife holds the key to the prison door. And she'll dangle that key for as long as it takes. That's your cue to apologize.

Those are three reasons why most acts of repentance are initiated by guys. You're guilty. You're altruistic. Or you've reached your limit.

It's worth noting that after your apology, she will often respond with her own apology. But it's not nearly as sincere or doesn't have quite the impact.

To be sure, we guys are experts at initiating closure. And that's exactly what our wives need us to do. Which means we are the ones ultimately in control. Yay for us.

So, the real question is not why guys apologize. But why we sometimes wait so long to do it. The answer might be that we take our time because we know the making up part is well worth the wait.

Takeaway

Warning: Please do not initiate a lovers' quarrel just because it's so fun to end a lovers' quarrel.

*"The end of argument or discussion should
be, not victory, but enlightenment."*
Joseph Joubert (1754–1824)

Wives Need Their Husbands...

To Trade His
Mustang for a Minivan

W hen I was in college, I remember making this statement more than once, "I will never live in a house with a white picket fence."

That was my way of taking a stand against the establishment. Sure, I knew I'd probably get married and have one or two kids. But a house in suburbia? With a picket fence? And a station wagon? And a lawn to mow and gutters to clean?

Not a chance. I was better than that.

For the record, I have never owned or erected a white picket fence. However, at the second house we owned, I came home from work one day to an image that could have rocked my world. My neighbor had installed a lovely and sturdy white picket fence—which meant the entire north side of my property now stood in mocking defiance of the personal pledge I had made ten years earlier.

But you know what? It was not a big deal. I looked at that fence and I laughed. By that time, I had three kids and had surrendered to the conformity and wonder of suburban life. I had not sold out. I had not turned my back on a freethinking rebellious countercultural lifestyle. Instead, I had found something better.

That's why a few years ago, I laughed again when I heard Andrew Peterson's song "Family Man." Andrew captured exactly what I had experienced with my growing family. Read the lyrics like a poem. And then, I recommend you track down the song itself.

I am a family man
I traded in my Mustang for a minivan
This is not what I was headed for when I began
This was not my plan
I am a family man

But everything I had to lose
Came back a thousand times in you
And you fill me up with love
Fill me up with love
And you help me stand
'Cause I am a family man

And life is good
That's something I always knew
But I just never understood
If you'd asked me then you know I'd say I never would
Settle down in a neighborhood
I never thought I could

But I don't remember anymore
Who I even was before
You filled me up with love
Filled me up with love
And you help me stand

So come on with the thunder clouds
Let the cold wind rail against us, let the rain come down
We can build a roof above us with the love we've found
We can stand our ground
So let the rain come down

Because love binds up what breaks in two
So keep my heart so close to you
And I'll fill you up with love
Fill you up with love
And I'll help you stand
'Cause I am a family man

I'm saving my vacation time
For Disneyland
This is not what I was headed for when I began

This was not my plan
It's so much better than*

The heart and message of the song are pretty clear, but allow me a moment of repetitive redundancy.

The song's hero had firmly committed to a life plan that did not include a neighborhood or a minivan. But the love of a good woman filled him a thousand times more than he ever expected. His unanticipated life is so good he doesn't even remember the old plan. Except he knows what he has now is even "better than."

Thanks, Andrew. What a privilege to have this song rambling around in my brain.

Takeaway

Never stop making big plans, but don't be surprised when your biggest plans and greatest successes grow out of family.

"How joyful and prosperous you will be! Your wife will be
like a fruitful grapevine, flourishing within your home. Your
children will be like vigorous young olive trees as they
sit around your table. That is the LORD's blessing."

PSALM 128:2-4 NLT

---

* ©2003 Andrew Peterson, from his album *Love and Thunder*. Lyrics printed by permission.

Wives Need Their Husbands...

To Rage Not

G uys who make a habit of getting angry are eager to point out that anger itself is not a bad thing. They say, "Hey, even Jesus got angry. Remember how he turned over the tables of the money changers in the temple?"

Gentlemen, you are absolutely correct. Plus, you get a gold star for quoting Scripture. But you didn't go quite far enough. You need to differentiate between righteous anger and selfish anger. Righteous anger is what Jesus modeled in John chapter 2. He didn't lose control. He saw the desecration of the temple and delivered a clear message: "How dare you turn my Father's house into a market!"

We should all feel righteous anger when facing such evils as child abuse, racism, abortion, and other injustices. In those cases, when kept under control, anger can be a force for good.

Selfish anger is often out of control. It's destructive. It's embarrassing. Have you ever gotten mad at an inanimate object? A vending machine, cell phone, or fishing pole? Did that anger help you retrieve your Snickers bar, reconnect your call, or get that fishing line untangled? Selfish anger prevents you from thinking straight. It's the opposite of thoughtfulness. Proverbs 14:29 says, "A patient man has great understanding, but a quick tempered man displays folly."

Worse, did you recently rage at someone you love? How did that turn out? In the moment, we feel justified in our anger. But that feeling doesn't last very long and we wish we could take it all back. Don't you wish there was a way to short-circuit those impulses that trigger your anger response? Wouldn't it be great if we could eliminate selfish anger all together? I don't think we can. The Bible also says, "In your anger do not sin" (Ephesians 4:26). That seems to suggest that anger is going to happen, but it's what we do with it that makes all the difference.

Digging a little deeper into Scripture, we get a pretty good plan for minimizing the damage of selfish anger. James 1:19-20 says, "Take note of this: Everyone should be quick to listen, slow to speak and slow to become angry, for man's anger does not bring about the righteous life that God desires."

When we begin to feel angry we need to see if we can lengthen the fuse. Take a moment before the explosion and consider the real cause of the anger, whether it really deserves such an outburst, and who's in our direct line of fire. It may sound corny, but it really may be a matter of counting to ten before we let loose. (Count slow enough and perhaps we won't have to let loose at all.)

One motivation for husbands to keep their anger in check is that we don't want to give our wives the satisfaction of saying things like "What are you so angry about?" or "Dude, chillax!" or worse, "You're embarrassing me." Of course, one of the reasons we have a wife is to hold us accountable and we should give her permission to correct us with gentleness and love. But still, it is never fun to hear that kind of sniping from our brides. Even when they're right. (Especially when they're right.)

The last reason to be slow to anger is because it allows us time to consider the bigger picture. Maybe what we're ticked off about is actually part of God's bigger plan for our life, but has not been revealed to us yet. We get angry when our home loan is turned down, but it saves us from buying a house that loses a third of its value in the recession. We get angry when our son gets cut from basketball, but that leads to new opportunities on the debate team. We get angry when we get passed over for promotion, but that would have moved our kids away from their grandparents.

There's a story about a man shipwrecked on a desert island. When a bolt of lightning destroys his primitive, handmade hut the man shakes his fist at heaven. Hours later he is stunned when the captain of a ship says, "We came because we saw your smoke signals."

Maybe the best way to prevent explosive, selfish anger is to make a heartfelt commitment to long-range, big-picture thinking. In other words, resolve to trust God's perfect plan.

Takeaway

You rage, you lose. Almost every time.

"A quick-tempered man does foolish things."
PROVERBS 14:17

Wives Need Their Husbands…

To Rebuild Love

I f something's missing from your marriage, maybe it's time to go back to the drawing board. To consider what forces forged loved in the first place. To go back to the basics. Back to boy meets girl.

Let's examine the stages that took you from first impression to marriage proposal and see which part of the relational assembly line has broken down. As any production manager will tell you, the factory output is only as efficient as its weakest link.

Attraction may be the first building block of love. What was it that attracted you to your bride in the first place? It could have been visual. A smile. Her eyes. The curve of some body part. Maybe you saw her walk or heard her laugh. You were drawn to her. Something sensual hit you. It might have been sudden. It might have been gradual. Spend a moment. Delight in that memory. Meditate on that first awareness of your attraction to your bride until it comes back. It's still there. Or it could be, if you want it to be.

Moving on. The second building block of love is *communication*. It may have been easy, it may have been awkward. Somehow the two of you started to make beautiful music together. There was a verbal chemistry including both small talk and real talk. Why did you care about what she was saying? Sure you wanted to kiss her. But at some point, you let down your guard. You talked about hopes and dreams. You cared about her family situation, her frustration, her fears. She asked questions and you answered honestly. You talked all night. That's when you knew. Can you still talk like that? Go ahead. Talk like that.

In the act of constructing love, what comes after looking and listening? *Respect.* Somehow that girlfriend of yours wasn't just a sex object. She wasn't just arm candy. You began to see all sides of her. Fun/serious. Intense/ easygoing. Spiritual/searching. Experienced/incomplete. Smart/gullible. A woman/a little girl. She became for you a puzzle, and unscrambling her secrets became a high priority. Do you still see the complete, complex woman? Or maybe you only see one side of her? Have you put her in a box? Or do you encourage your bride to explore her many sides and many gifts? That's respect.

When you finally see who she is, then you begin to see what she needs. That's when guys do our best work. As men, we have the answers. We fill in the blanks. We need to be needed. *Provision.* Financial provision and more. As a couple, you are at your best when you are filling her every need. We are the hunters, the cabin builders, the fire starters. We are the providers. If that role has been taken away from you, then don't be surprised if you feel like less of a man.

Closely tied with provision is *protection.* We don't just slay wild animals for food. We keep the wolves and grizzlies from the door. We man the watch-tower. We lock the doors at night with a satisfying click. We swing away at the prowler. We sit on the couch and our bride slides next to us, under our arm, and she puts her head on our chest. When needed, we rise up with incredible latent power. Like a knight in shining armor, we rescue and protect.

Finally, when we find a woman worthy of all of the above, we have one more step to take, one more decision to make. *Exclusivity.* That's when we can bring our laserlike focus onto the goal of uniting with one woman for the rest of our lives.

I would never attempt to define love. But these elements come pretty close to describing how love should act. *Attraction, communication, respect, provision, protection, exclusivity.*

Husbands, are you falling short in any of these areas? (I'm talking to you, not your wife.) If there's work to be done, take personal responsibility for strengthening that particular foundational piece of your relationship. See if your entire marriage isn't stronger because of your intentional, sacrificial commitment to love.

Takeaway

Fast-forward through the memories of 20 events from your first meeting to your marriage proposal. Share the best of those memories with your bride. Over dinner. During a walk. Cuddling in bed. Or in a letter.

> *"Love at first sight is easy to understand; it's when people have been looking at each other for a lifetime that it becomes a miracle."*
> SAM LEVENSON (1911–1980)

Wives Need Their Husbands…

To Not Share This List with Your Wife

I apologize in advance for this chapter. It was way too easy to write. And all it does is perpetuate the myth that guys are animals and women are either ditzy or nags or both. These supposed truths are easy punch lines for most sitcoms, second-rate comedians, and comic strips when the topic is marriage.

You may laugh at this list. But I hope you also discover the hidden message for both husbands and wives.

I present the differences between men and women:

- Men like the Three Stooges. Women are Stooge haters.

- Men look at a color swatch and say "blue." Women look at the same color swatch and say "periwinkle" or "navy" or "turquoise" or "teal" or "cobalt."

- Women are always ready to share their thoughts and feelings, sometimes with tears. Men grunt.

- Women love chocolate. Men (smart ones) buy it for them.

- Women love cats. Men love dogs. When women are around, men might say they love cats, but when they are alone, there is an increase in cat-kicking.

- Women love children. Men sometimes acknowledge the existence of short people living in the house.

- Women expect men to change. Men don't change.

- Men say the first thing they notice about a woman is her eyes. Women know that's a lie.

- Some men look good in a mustache. No women look good in a mustache.

- Women dot their "i's" with hearts and end handwritten notes with smiley faces. Men don't use pens or pencils anymore.

- Women look in the mirror and hate what they see. Men look in the mirror, suck in their tummy, flex, and say, "Not bad. Not bad at all" or "Still got it." Even if they never had it.

- Men's brains are 12 percent bigger than women's brains. Enough said.

- Women are embarrassed by flatulence. Men are amused by flatulence.

- Men own 3 pairs of shoes. Women own between 4 and 400 pairs.

- Men's haircuts cost $14. Plus $1 tip. Women's haircuts cost $75. Plus $10 tip.

- Women make their beds in hotels. Men don't know why women do this.

- Women feel empowered through emotional support from a loving husband. Men feel empowered by a full tank of gas and $300 cash in their wallet.

- Men clean up the kitchen and expect several minutes of praise. Women clean up the kitchen because it's their job.

- Women pile things at the bottom of the stairs as a reminder to take them up on the next trip. Men step over those things.

- Men forget birthdays and anniversaries. Women should accept this fact by now.

Did you laugh? Don't feel guilty.

The single inarguable point to remember is this. Men and women are different. Most jokes have some kernel of truth. Otherwise there's no comedic value.

So, guys. Laugh. Appreciate and even celebrate the differences. Be a little more understanding. And only dare to share this list with your wife when she's in a real good mood.

Takeaway

There can be no victor in the battle of the sexes.

> *"A good marriage would be between*
> *a blind wife and a deaf husband."*
>
> MONTAIGNE (1533–1592)

Wives Need Their Husbands...

To Share This List with Your Wife

A little research actually went into this chapter. Hopefully, the list of facts below will help you better understand the wonderful, mysterious, tempting creature who shares your life and bed.

I apologize for not documenting each of these facts below, but they won't need confirmation. In your heart you know they're accurate.

I present the fact-based differences between men and women:*

- While speaking, women maintain eye contact for an average of 12 seconds. Men glance away, on average, every 3 seconds.

- Men speak 12,500 words every day. Women speak twice that.

- Men use the left side of their brain more (problem-solving, task-oriented). Women use the right side of their brain more (feelings, creativity).

- Men's brains are 12 percent bigger than women's brains. But only because they need more neurons to control their greater muscle mass and body size.

- Men process language in one hemisphere of their brain. Women process language on both sides of their brain. That's one of the reasons women's language skills tend to recover more quickly after a stroke.

- The inferior-parietal lobule, which is thought to control mathematical ability, is significantly larger in men.

---

* www.mastersofhealthcare.com/blog/2009/10-big-differences-between-mens-and-womens-brains/.

- Women have larger kidneys, liver, stomach, and appendix, but smaller lungs.

- Women have a thicker parietal region in their brain, which limits their ability to mentally rotate objects in their brains. Men can look at an object and literally see the other side.

- Women have a larger deep limbic system, which promotes bonding and puts them in touch with their feelings, but which also makes them more susceptible to depression.

- Men are approximately three times more likely to commit suicide (Royal College of Psychiatrists).

- Men are four times more likely to die of a smoking-related disease (World Health Organization).

- Men are 2.7 times more likely to be in a car accident (World Health Organization).

Did you learn something? Probably not. It turns out that once you've been married a few years, there's not much that can really surprise you about the opposite sex. It's just nice that many of the differences are based on actual observation, not on conjecture and myth.

So guys, feelings do matter more for your bride. They do have superior verbal skills. You are better at math, spatial relationships, and problem-solving. And even though she may be more likely to be depressed, you are more likely to commit suicide. Be careful out there.

Takeaway

Pity the scientists who devote their lives to topics like coleopterology or paleopedology. The study of beetles or ancient soils could not be nearly as fascinating as the study of the female sex.

"The LORD God said, 'It is not good for the man to be alone. I will make a helper suitable for him.'"

GENESIS 2:18

Wives Need Their Husbands…

To Not Be the Jerk in the Stands

I'm a good husband and a good dad.

Except at my kids' games and matches. I confess. I am the jerk in the stands.

Even as I type this, you need to know that I'm not at all making light of it. I'm not shrugging it off as just an eccentricity. I am not excusing my behavior. Regretfully, I am not claiming total victory over it. True, I am actually better than I was years ago, but still I stomp around sidelines, mutter under my breath, yell at umpires and referees, and embarrass my wife and kids.

That's the worst part. I've spent thousands of hours in bleachers, lawn chairs, and leaning against fences. And I can't bear to think how many of those hours members of my own family have been regretting that I was there. How stupid am I?

In my head I can replay images of the way I have acted, and it's more than a little frustrating. It's almost like an out-of-body experience. I ask myself, *Who is this guy? Why is he making such a fool of himself?*

To be clear, I don't yell negative words at my kids or any of the young athletes. It's mostly at refs. Sometimes at the situation. Often my comments are just over-the-top, loud game analysis. Frustration boiling over. Many times I'm aggressively voicing what many of the other fans are thinking. But like my wife reminds me, "Jay, your voice carries." Which I hate to hear, but need to hear.

Which, of course, is the point. When husbands screw up, we need to give our wives permission to correct us. If I'm a jerk and Rita calls me on it, I cannot respond by being even more of a jerk.

Other examples. If we husbands are rude to a waiter or clerk, we want our wife to let us know. If your body odor is nasty, you want your wife to let you know. If we park in a tow zone or on the neighbor's grass, we want her to tell us. If I'm about to track mud into my boss's house, if I'm talking loudly on my cell phone or holding up a long line at a ticket counter for a measly 84 cents, I want my wife to gently point out how my action could be improved. It may not be pleasant to hear, but that's part of her job and I need to let her do it.

If I really buy into this idea, I need to actually request her intervention. Now that takes a real man, but maybe you're ready to swallow your pride and ask for her help.

Over the years, Rita and I have tried a variety of strategies to minimize my jerk-in-the-stand scenarios. We've talked about it. We've prayed about it. I've given her permission to nudge me if I start acting up. I've learned to walk down to the foul pole or end zone when I feel the need to voice my loud opinions. I've gripped sharp key rings for entire basketball games as a reminder to shut the heck up. I've stood with other dads who yell even more than me. I've distracted myself with game-day responsibilities like videotaping, working chain gang or concession stand, and even doing the umping myself.

Some strategies work better than others. Like I said, I'm better than I used to be. I will never forget my outbursts during one of Alec's baseball games in Lombard and one of Randy's wrestling matches in Sycamore. Those both took place more than a decade ago, and I still cringe when I drive past that baseball diamond and that high-school gym.

So that's my one fatal flaw. I have others, but being a jerk in the stand is the big one. What's yours? It may have nothing to do with being loud or boorish. It may be your habit of laying on guilt or shirking responsibility, your perfectionism, your lack of trust, or the need to always be right. A quick review of the seven deadly sins may reveal that you are over the top when it comes to greed, sloth, envy, wrath, pride, lust, or gluttony.

What's your strategy for fixing your regretful condition? Here's a hint: You can't do it on your own. You're going to need the help of your wife and your Creator. Go ahead. Ask both of them to help. And then…let them.

Takeaway

It's difficult to admit when we're wrong. It's even more difficult to admit that we can't admit that we're wrong.

*"Those who disregard discipline despise themselves, but
the one who heeds correction gains understanding."*
Proverbs 15:32

Wives Need Their Husbands...

To Do the Church Thing

This Sunday, 13 million more women will attend church than men. Why? Well, there's no shortage of excuses.

"I've got an 8 a.m. tee time."

"The Packers play at noon."

"Sunday is my one day off."

"The pastor rubs me the wrong way."

"The church is full of hypocrites."

"I tried it. It just wasn't my style."

"I don't have to go to a building to spend time with God."

You can probably come up with a few good ones yourself. But I think the number-one reason guys aren't drawn to church is because it feels like surrender. The church experience is kind of wimpy. The music is sentimental. The people are all a little too nice. The theme of most Sunday sermons is, Do nice things and don't do bad things.

Guys don't want to be told to be nice. They want to hang out in a place where they can flex their muscles, spit, adjust their jockstraps, and rescue an occasional damsel in distress. Especially on weekends! Many guys spend all week saying "yes" to their bosses and customers. On the weekend, they want to be bold and courageous and to change the world.

Well, gentlemen, if your local church is making you feel like a girlie man, then you have two choices. Find a new church that teaches true biblical manhood. Or an even better idea is to get proactively involved in making your current church a place where men feel challenged and empowered.

Before we go too much further, allow me to affirm that Christianity is not for wimps. For the first 30 years of his life, Jesus was a carpenter. He had calloused hands and knew how to swing a hammer. At least four of the apostles were fishermen, not a job for lightweights. Eleven of the apostles were martyred for following Jesus, very likely enduring all manner of beatings and torture before their executions.

When it comes to physical strength, Paul wrote to the Corinthians that a well-disciplined body was a priority for his work as an evangelist.

> I discipline my body like an athlete, training it to do what it should. Otherwise, I fear that after preaching to others I myself might be disqualified (1 Corinthians 9:27 NLT).

Physical training was imperative to Paul because he knew the enemy was not to be taken lightly.

> Be strong in the Lord and in his mighty power. Put on the full armor of God, so that you can take your stand against the devil's schemes. For our struggle is not against flesh and blood, but against the rulers, against the authorities, against the powers of this dark world and against the spiritual forces of evil in the heavenly realms (Ephesians 6:10-12).

Plus, we are not responsible for just ourselves. The book of Romans tells us we need strength in order to take care of those who cannot fend for themselves.

> We who are strong ought to bear the weaknesses of those without strength and not just please ourselves (Romans 15:1 NASB).

Despite what many hymns suggest, Jesus was not meek and mild. He called the Pharisees vipers to their faces. He drove the money changers from the temple. Before he died, he endured flogging of a kind so severe that it killed other men and then carried his own cross up a mountain. Revelation tells us he will return on horseback brandishing a sword of judgment.

Following Jesus is not for the weak or timid. You—and all the men of your church—would do well to meet regularly, sing songs of courage, listen to teachings specific to men's issues, and challenge each other to do great things for your community and the world.

Such as? Build churches in mission fields. Rehab homes for single moms and the elderly. Share the gospel with men in prison. Visit VA hospitals, listen to war heroes, and pray for them and their families. Arrange motorcycle escorts for returning soldiers. Get in the faces of fathers who have abandoned their responsibilities and tell them to be the dads their kids need. Volunteer to coach basketball or soccer for boys who desperately need mentors and direction in their lives. Fast for 48 hours. Pray courageously. Read Scripture aloud in rich, resonant, gravelly voices.

What's your excuse now, guys? Spend a few minutes kicking around ideas and you'll come up with a long list of kingdom-building activities that require vast amounts of testosterone. Or maybe you're not man enough.

Just to be fair. Jesus did have a gentle side. He wept. He washed the feet of the disciples. He said, "Let the little children come to me." He was called "the lamb of God."

So don't be too quick to say strength is good and gentleness is bad. What we should be saying is Christ is our model in all things and all ways. He is the Lion of Judah, Lamb of God, Good Shepherd, High Priest, Bridegroom, Prince of Peace, Rose of Sharon, Living Water, Rock, Door, Judge, True Vine, Bright Morning Star, and the Way, the Truth, and the Life.

By the way, in God's eyes surrender is not a bad thing. The authentic Christian life is a surrendered life of putting others first. If your goal is greatness, Jesus can model that as well.

> Whoever wants to become great among you must be your servant, and whoever wants to be first must be your slave—just as the Son of Man did not come to be served, but to serve, and to give his life as a ransom for many (Matthew 20:26-28).

Guys, I hope you're out of excuses now. You belong in active fellowship with a group of authentic believers. Don't go to church for your wife. Don't go to church for your kids. Go to church for you. And for God. He doesn't need your help. But he'll use you to build the kingdom in ways you can't imagine.

Takeaway

It takes strength to be gentle. It takes courage to surrender. It takes a real man to lead his family in worship on Sunday morning.

"There has got abroad a notion, somehow, that if you become a Christian you must sink your manliness and turn milksop."
CHARLES SPURGEON (1834–1892)

Wives Need Their Husbands…

To Get Dirty Together with Her

Sometimes your wife is most adorable when she has just come in from gardening, finished wallpapering the kids' bedroom, or sprinted home from the park pushing your toddler in one of those jogging strollers. There's a little perspiration around her neckline, a smudge on her cheek, and a glow that seems to surround her. It's a good look. It's raw, earthy, real. It's an important image for wives to project once in a while. And husbands too.

In our house we call it the "Saturday look." Dirt, sweat, and paint stains earned in the battle of building a home and family are like medals of honor. It's good honest dirt. It's proof that your family's values extend beyond the pages of *Mademoiselle* and *GQ*. The honeymoon is over (in a good way). You're a hard-working husband-and-wife team. You're not afraid of a little sweat, and you're not hung up on outward appearances.

The ability to get dirty opens all kinds of creative and constructive possibilities. Getting dirty with your bride has added bonuses you haven't even thought of. Projects get done twice as fast or faster. The two of you experience dialogue with a purpose. Working together on a project assures that you both have input and neither is surprised by the creative choices. Later, that new fence, the revitalized patio, the clean garage, the gleaming tile, the home-grown veggies, or the refinished kitchen cabinets will bring surprising satisfaction because you invested more than cash. You invested yourself.

Don't forget how traditional male-female roles tend to surface in these kinds of projects. What man doesn't want to say, "Need that stump removed? Out of my way, little lady. My trusty axe and I have work to do." Of course, my wife certainly loves to order me around hauling flats of flowers. "Bring the tray of petunias here. Oh my goodness, those are impatiens for the shade.

I said bring me petunias for the sun." Funny thing, my feelings are not hurt at all that I don't know the difference between petunias, impatiens, or daffodils. And I certainly don't know which ones need shade or sun.

What I do care about is that together we're getting dirty.

Other short-term benefits include demonstrating manual labor to your kids, increasing your property value, catching some rays, sharing a glass of lemonade, and kissing a drop of sweat off your bride's nose. If some hose spray goes astray, that's all part of the plan.

One of the best parts of the "Saturday look" is that it precedes Saturday night. As the afternoon morphs into evening, it's time to wash away that good honest dirt. If you and your wife happen to bump into each other before, during, or after that shower, then the "Saturday look" takes on an entirely different meaning.

Feeling refreshed, you can put on some fresh jeans and a shirt with buttons. Maybe a jacket. Drop the kids at Mom's. Linger over pasta and tiramisu at your favorite Italian restaurant. Talk about hopes and dreams for next year or just for next Saturday.

I probably don't need to go much further with this chapter. I think—and I hope—you can take it from here.

----------------- **Takeaway** -----------------

Full disclosure: Rita and I have agreed to never wallpaper together again. Too much conflict. But other than that, we're pretty good at sharing the "Saturday look."

"There is no more lovely, friendly, and charming relationship,
communion, or company than a good marriage."
Martin Luther (1483–1546)

Wives Need Their Husbands...

To Do More Than Nod and Smile

You're at the kitchen table. She's talking. You're listening. You're taking it all in. She's making sense. You sincerely care what she's talking about. You're even nodding in agreement and adding a thoughtful verbal response every now and then.

Then, disaster.

For some reason your mind wanders. Maybe something she said triggered thoughts of an old girlfriend. Maybe a TV in the background mentioned a player on your fantasy football team. Maybe your stomach reminded you that you hadn't eaten in ninety minutes. You've effectively tuned her out for the last one to seven minutes. Worst of all, you're still nodding and responding with affirmative grunts.

She wraps up her verbal proposal and says something that requires a response. Something like, "Does that make sense?" or "Can you do that?" or "How does next Thursday sound?" And now you need to respond.

When we realize what is happening, all guys do the same thing. Our mushy, unfocused minds become keenly aware of any clues pertaining to what our wives might be talking about. We do a two-second inventory of our immediate surroundings. Is she holding theater tickets, an IRS bulletin, a brochure from a cruise line, an e-mail from the high-school dean, a sales receipt from Old Navy? You search your recent memory banks to see if somehow you can recall a train of thought from before your mind wandered. You strain your brain to catch a few stray words that are still lingering in the air or that made it into your ear canals but have not yet been deleted. If you're lucky, her pen is poised over a date on her calendar. Or her laptop is open to a page that has all the information you need to continue the conversation without admitting to your wandering cerebrum. But more than half the time, you really have no idea how to respond.

What are your choices? "Yes." "No." "Let me think about it." Or tap dance.

I can't recommend a total positive or total negative response. You may be agreeing to something that costs you many dollars or many hours that you just don't want to invest.

"Let me think about it" is not a bad strategy. It's noncommittal. It delays your response until you can survey clues, gain additional data, and actually answer the question that was posed. It may also sidestep the entire question, allowing the issue to work itself out. The risk is that your wife might say, "What is there to think about?" and then you're stuck.

I've become pretty good at verbal tap dancing over the years. The strategy is to hesitantly deliver short, nonspecific unfinished statements that may lead your wife to add more information until the original question becomes clear. Things like "Well…" "I…uh…" "That would…" You need to stretch your acting muscles to make this work. But if you look like you're really pondering the question and all its implications, she will continue the discussion without you and very likely give you plenty of clues to catch up and catch on. The tap-dance strategy is a true art form and not for the squeamish or faint of heart. You need to commit to it and not back down. If your wife knows you're tap dancing, you're in for a real tough morning.

Which brings me to the fifth and best option. Confess, apologize, and give her the answer she wants to hear.

You see, as good as I am at tap dancing, Rita has become even better at detecting it. It's a product of the thousands of conversations we've had over the years. She'll call my bluff even before I begin. She knows the signs and will never hesitate to say, "You're not listening, are you?" As terrible as those words are to hear, they are really a blessing. A quick confession and short apology will move the conversation to where it should already be going. Don't make a big deal about the apology and maybe even add a chuckle if possible. Something like, "Sorry, I was distracted for a moment. What was that last thing you said?" A smart wife (Rita) won't berate her husband, because she knows she has the upper hand. She will simply restate the question and include obvious hints that guide the husband toward the answer she wants to hear.

In summary. Listen to your bride. If your mind wanders, the world doesn't end. But there's a good chance you'll end up doing it her way. Which probably is the best choice anyway.

Takeaway

When you make a small misstep, your next move should be to take a step back and get on the right path. If you keep walking like nothing happened, you may be lost for-ev-er.

"When a woman is talking to you,
listen to what she says with her eyes."

VICTOR HUGO (1802–1885)

Wives Need Their Husbands...

To Stir Her Pots

I stir Rita's pots.

No, that's not a euphemism for some exciting new bedroom maneuver. (I wish.) What I mean is that I literally stir her pots. When there's something on the stove—mashed potatoes, minestrone soup, a vegetable medley—I cannot help myself. I grab a wooden spoon and start swirling. Why? I'm not sure.

It's certainly not that I think she needs my help. She's a fine cook. She doesn't need me to rescue her recipes. Perhaps it's my way of checking the dinner schedule. Or maybe I'm whetting my appetite for the dinner she's preparing for our family. Stirring the pot wafts the delicious aroma of tonight's stew or soup into the kitchen and beyond. If I dig deep into my subconscious, I suppose it could be that I'm just making sure the bottom of the pot doesn't burn. Or maybe I'm checking to see if the concoction needs a dash of this or a dollop of that. I do prefer things spicier than my bride. But I maintain that I am not checking up on her or questioning her cooking prowess.

How does Rita respond to my involuntary stirring sessions? The first 99 times I stirred her pot, she wasn't happy. She seemed to question my motives. I was infringing on her territory, and perhaps she even felt threatened. I was in her space and she let me know it. Sometimes verbally and sometimes non-verbally.

How did I respond to her justifiable retaliation? I was mostly clueless. My response was pretty much, "What's the big deal? It's a pot. It's just a stir. There's no law against it. There's no malicious intent. Why do you feel so threatened?"

Uh-oh. Now what? (Husbands, if you think you know where this is going, think again.)

This book by design is filled with many lessons for husbands that lead to changed behavior. If you do something stupid, apologize. If you do something hurtful, apologize and don't ever do it again. If your wife has a need, fill it. And so on.

But guess what happened when I stirred Rita's pot for the hundredth time? She got used to it.

Sure she still noticed. She rolled her eyes or let out a breath of exasperation. Sometimes she had a snide remark. But it always came with a smile. Around my hundredth pot stir, she realized there was no threat and no ulterior motive.

For my bride, somehow my pot-stirring morphed from frustrating to endearing. Yay for me. Yay for Rita for sticking around long enough that she learned to live with and even love my quirky eccentricities.

Now of course, this chapter really has nothing to do with spoons or pots. It has everything to do with sticking around. It's about looking past the annoying habits. It's about priorities and possibilities. Believe it or not, those little aggravations can add up—not to grounds for divorce based on irreconcilable differences—but to moments of loving appreciation for your spouse as an individual. Flaws and all.

Years from now, if I die before Rita—and I hope I do—I like to think that she'll have something on the stove and will pick up a wooden spoon and smile thinking about me and my pesky old habit. I hope she gives that pot an extra stir, just for me.

Takeaway

No husband or wife has permission to be annoying. But we must give each other permission to be real.

"The art of being wise is the art of knowing what to overlook."
William James (1842–1910)

Wives Need Their Husbands…

To Get Love Right

Prepare to be slightly confused. Love can do that to you. Probably because there are so many different kinds of love.

Romantic love is tough for guys because we get all hung up somewhere between sappy poetry and primal urges. Brotherly love is what you share with teammates, roommates, and guys in your small group. *Love* is also a word we use—probably in error—to describe various relationships with our cars, pizza, the NBA, and our most recent iTunes download.

Dig out your New Testament Greek dictionary and you'll find words like *agape*, which is a sacrificial kind of love. The example of the Good Samaritan might help with that definition—going out of your way for someone without expecting anything in return.

Researching this topic, I ran across a Greek word I had not seen before: *storge*. It is apparently love shared within a family, including between a parent and child. *Storge* love may also include those physical expressions of affection that our wives crave in vast amounts, but that DON'T lead to sex. A hug, a kiss, holding hands. The need for *storge* love is more proof that boys and girls are different.

Jesus is very explicit about our need to love. The Pharisees tested him with the question, "Which is the greatest commandment in the law?" Jesus replied, "'Love the Lord your God with all your heart and with all your soul and with all your mind.' This is the first and greatest commandment. And the second is like it: 'Love your neighbor as yourself'" (Matthew 22:35-39).

But there's more. Beyond the requirement to love God and love our neighbor, Jesus also says to "love your enemies" (Matthew 5:44). Proverbs tells us "a friend loves at all times" (Proverbs 17:17).

Then, there's the love God has for every human on the planet as described in John 3:16. The fact that God sent his son to pay the price for our sins is a truth we need to hold in our hearts even though it is beyond the scope of our comprehension.

What has become known as the "love chapter" of the Bible—1 Corinthians chapter 13—has a helpful analysis of how love needs to act. You've undoubtedly seen the words framed, calligraphed, and posterized. I'm pretty sure Rita and I received about five variations as wedding gifts.

> Love is patient, love is kind. It does not envy, it does not boast, it is not proud. It does not dishonor others, it is not self-seeking, it is not easily angered, it keeps no record of wrongs. Love does not delight in evil but rejoices with the truth. It always protects, always trusts, always hopes, always perseveres. Love never fails (1 Corinthians 13:4-8).

That's a great list. I recommend you use it as a checklist to see if you are acting loving toward your wife, neighbors, co-workers, friends, family, and even your enemies. Still, it's not a definition. The love chapter describes what love does, not really what love is.

The mystery, I believe, is solved in 1 John, one of the last books of the Bible. When you get a chance, read all of 1 John—it's only about four or five pages long. Right now, consider this short excerpt:

> We know and rely on the love God has for us. God is love. Whoever lives in love lives in God, and God in them (1 John 4:16).

Did you catch that? God is Love. If you know God, you know love. If you don't know him, you can't really expect to love in any way, shape, or form. I hope that doesn't surprise you. But, I also hope it inspires you to dig deeper and love without hesitation. With your wife, that means loving sacrificially, unconditionally, romantically, and yes, erotically.

Because I don't want to get in trouble with any theologians out there, I must quickly add this disclaimer. Please don't put God in a box labeled "love." Indeed, God is love. Absolutely. But add to that. God is Truth. God is Justice. God is Life. God is Mercy. God is Righteousness.

All of which reminds me of the statement by the controversial theologian, David Jenkins, bishop of Durham. "No statement about God is simply, literally true. God is far more than can be measured, described, defined in ordinary language, or pinned down to any particular happening."

Takeaway

Don't fear love. Don't be afraid to say the word, to sift through the disguises of love, even to surrender completely to the knowledge and feeling of love.

"Dear friends, let us love one another, for love comes from God. Everyone who loves has been born of God and knows God."

1 JOHN 4:7

Wives Need Their Husbands…

To Make Jay's
Winter Chicken Soup

The days are gone when wives planned, shopped, cooked, and served 365 suppers at home per year. Every family is different, but I'm going to assume that in your home that number is still somewhere close to 200. Pizza delivery, Chinese carryout, Colonel chicken, McDs, nicer restaurants, holidays, skipped meals, sports banquets, tailgating, weddings, and dinner at grandma's account for the other evenings. You may try to take credit for the days that you play grill master, but please don't. Chances are your bride arranged for the buns, side dishes, relishes, and condiments. All you did was burn the burgers or undercook the pork chops, giving everyone a fun salmonella scare.

After 30 years of marriage, I am stunned to consider that Rita may very well have called the kids and me to the table some 6000 times. That's a lot of spaghetti, pot roasts, baked tilapia, stir fry, tacos, and tuna casserole.

That's also a lot of me saying, "Great dinner. Thanks, love." But somehow, that doesn't quite seem like enough. Which is why guys need a strategy and a go-to recipe that allows us—once every few weeks—to be hero for the day. Here's the plan…

First, pick an evening or afternoon that your wife looks a little haggard. (Don't tell her she looks haggard. Trust me, that would be totally counterproductive.) Also, make sure she isn't already defrosting something. Then, offhandedly say, "Hey, can I make dinner tonight?" Her response might be a quizzical look, an enthusiastic cheer, an outright guffaw, or a sarcastic verbal response. Something like, "Wow, that would be great. What are we having? Toast?" With the recipe below you can honestly and casually say, "I have something a little more satisfying and nutritious in mind, but thanks for the vote of confidence."

Then, go shopping. Check to see if you already have potatoes, an onion, or anything else on the list. But don't involve your wife too much. If she has to get up from her comfy chair five times to look for veggies, find a big pot, point you to the spice cabinet, or show you how to turn on the stove, you're totally defeating the purpose.

Here's the plan. I hope you can take it from here.

Jay's Winter Chicken Soup

GAME PARTS:

One of those hot, precooked chickens popular now in supermarket delis for about $6.99

A can of chicken broth or five or six chicken bouillon cubes

A half bag of those small carrots with the rounded edges

Two big potatoes or four small potatoes (rinsed)

An onion

A couple of stalks of celery, if you like

A nice handful of egg noodles (not as many as you think, because they expand like crazy as they cook)

A few good dashes of garlic powder or one of those Italian seasoning blends that include basil, oregano, parsley, sage, rosemary, and thyme

A few cups of water

A nice, fresh warm loaf of French or Italian bread from the same supermarket (the kind of bread that comes in the long, white paper bag)

GAME PLAN:

At home, wash your hands, plop the bird on a cutting board, and start pulling off chunks of meat. Cut the chicken chunks, carrots, onion, potatoes, and celery into pieces. Any size works. I usually chop everything to about the size of a sugar cube. For sure peel the onion, but you can even leave the skin on the potatoes.

Put everything in a big pot except the noodles (and the bread). Get that water boiling. And then toss in the noodles. Check the directions on the bag of noodles, but 10 to 12 minutes should do it. Stir a lot. Simmer (which means turn down the heat) while you cut the bread into nice thick one-inch slices. Serve!

A couple of other hints. Clean as you go. Taste the broth and toss in spices until you like it. Don't burn your tongue. Set the table with soup spoons, butter knives, bowls, and bread plates. If there's any left over, just leave it on the stove to cool and make room in the fridge for the entire pot. Insist that you also clean up the kitchen.

Finally, guys, deflect any praise. Do not assume or accept hero status for making one measly meal. Making a pot of soup once every couple of months is no big deal.

Takeaway

There's great insight in doing what she does. And in her doing what you do. Once in a while.

"Cooking is like love. It should be entered into with abandon or not at all."
HARRIET VAN HORNE (1920–1998)

Wives Need Their Husbands…

To Hold Her Book Up on Television

'm watching *Late Night with David Letterman* and Jerry Seinfeld is on the couch chatting with Dave about his latest project. At the end of his segment, Dave holds up a cookbook written by Jerry's wife. It's one of those celebrity fund-raising things. There's nothing special about it. I'm sure there are a few tasty recipes in its pages. But, if you want a cookbook there are better choices. The classic *Better Homes and Gardens Cookbook* covers everything you need to know in the kitchen, from proper egg-scrambling technique to how to keep the edges of a pie crust from overbrowning. Churches and school groups regularly publish collections of favorite recipes as fund-raisers, and that money stays right in your hometown. At the very least, your next cookbook purchase should be written by an actual chef, not a celebrity wife. But that's not the point of this chapter.

The point is this. Just before they go to commercial, Jerry grabs the cookbook out of Letterman's hands and holds it up to the camera. It's kind of an awkward moment. Watching it, you can't help but wonder why two multimillionaire entertainers are wasting time on national television with such a trivial matter. Then suddenly it all makes sense. Jerry says, "My wife told me to hold it." Well done, Mr. Seinfeld.

Mrs. Seinfeld had a "project." She made a reasonable request of her husband. It was something that was slightly awkward, but not impossible. He could have said, "Honey, holding up your cookbook is not really appropriate." But instead, Jerry chose to do the wise husband thing.

Gentlemen, most of the time I urge you to follow Jerry's lead. When your bride makes a request, just go with it. Not always, but almost always, do the wise husband thing. Examples?

You are absolutely positive that no one cares about the height of your sweat socks. (Anklets, footies, crew, over-the-calf. Whatever.) But if she suggests a certain sock style with your hiker shorts, just wear it.

You are already on your way to bed when your bride reminds you that tomorrow is trash collection day. You are quite confident that there's plenty of time in the morning, but for some reason she suggests you take the cans to the curb tonight. Without any wisecracks or grumbling, just curb it.

You are in charge of the fund-raiser for the citywide soccer program—selling dinner coupons for local restaurants—and you've got your entire presentation worked out. On the way to the meeting, she asks you also to mention the spirit-wear table she has helped organize. You are certain that talking about caps and T-shirts will take focus away from the main fund-raiser. My recommendation? Just say it.

I have no facts to back this up, but Jerry's follow-through on behalf of Mrs. Seinfeld that night probably sold several thousand cookbooks for whatever cause they were supporting. I hope it was a worthy one.

Likewise, following your own wife's requests almost always works out for the best as well. Surrendering to her sock selection may save you from a summer of embarrassing tan lines on your calves. When the trash collectors come down the street earlier than usual the next morning, you don't have to jump out of bed and drag the cans to the street in your jammies. When the spirit-wear table makes an extra two grand for the soccer club, you can take all the credit because of your eloquent pitch. It's a win-win. (And we like win-wins.)

Guys, I'm not saying you blindly do everything your wife asks. If there's a reason to talk it out, then talk it out. But—come on. You know she'll usually win the argument and, besides, her judgment is usually spot on. She picked you for a husband, didn't she?

Takeaway

When she makes a specific request, don't say no until you've considered her perspective and your motivations.

"Man has his will—but woman has her way."
Oliver Wendell Holmes Sr. (1809–1894)

Wives Need Their Husbands...

To Be the Dad

I f you're a dad, you probably remember that feeling of being out of the loop for about a year. During your wife's pregnancy and your newborn's first few months of life, it was not about you. It was about them. Mom and baby had a wonderful little connection—physical, emotional, spiritual—and you were on the outside looking in.

Finally it became your turn. It was time for you to step up and be the dad. Your new kid needed you. Your wife needed you. How did you do? Did you become part of their world? Did the three of you become a family? All for one and one for all? Or did you build walls and remain on the outside looking in? Maybe you bought into the common misconception that "fatherhood is grueling years of thankless toil." That idea is a dangerous and disappointing distortion.

Not long ago, I sat in the back of a parenting seminar and watched some guy billed as an "internationally known expert" point fingers, agonize, accuse, and yell for 45 minutes about the importance of reasserting parental authority and keeping your kids in line. The guy was occasionally entertaining, but his core message was mean-spirited and depressing.

Not once did I hear him talk about the joy of fatherhood. Not once did I get the sense he ever laughed with his kids. He talked a lot about tough love. But not much about unconditional love.

I cannot recall any of his memorized jokes, but the punch lines all seemed to center on how kids are "more trouble than they're worth." In his world, teenagers and parents never have a civil adult conversation about life, current events, weekend plans, college plans, friends, hopes, or dreams.

The speaker characterized parenting as "us" against "them." Kids are a burden. Kids are a problem that needs to be solved.

Thankfully, the Bible says just the opposite. Psalm 127 is inspiring in its imagery and clear mandate for fathers.

> Children are a gift from the LORD; they are a reward from him. Children born to a young man are like arrows in a warrior's hands. How joyful is the man whose quiver is full of them! (Psalm 127:3-5 NLT).

Men, you bring parenting skills to the table that the mother of your children just doesn't have. Gather those arrows. Sharpen them. Hone them with care so they are straight and true. Pull them close with love, respect, and clear instruction. Help them choose a target just right for them. Then allow them to fly into the world with grace and purpose. That's what a dad does.

Let me be clear. Does being a dad take time? Yes. Lots of it.

Are there moments when you have to use every ounce of your brainpower and expend great physical energy to meet a challenge presented by one of your kids? Yes.

Is there heartache and sleepless nights? Yes.

Do you need to coordinate strategies with your children's mother, share tactics with other dads, read books, and pray fervently? Yes.

But is it a burden, a thankless toil? No.

Instead, think of it as a quest. A puzzle. Being a father is a journey of discovery and wonderment. If you accept the challenge and pursue wise solutions, then great rewards come early and often. Stay in the game and dividends keep coming for the rest of your life.

Incredibly, you'll find joy, purpose and meaning in every phase:

- anxious pregnancies,
- exhausting labor and delivery,
- 2 a.m. feedings,
- the so-called "terrible twos" (which is really an amazing year),
- the grade-school years of self-discovery,
- the blossoming tween years,
- the teenage years when you begin to connect with your kids on an adult level,
- the college years when kids realize how much you have sacrificed for them,

- early career counseling when they sincerely ask your advice,
- emotionally charged wedding plans,
- grandparenting, and beyond.

Each phase comes with wonderful, memorable moments for men whom God has chosen to be a father. Make sense? I hope so. If the rewards aren't coming as often as you might like, stick with it. Be there, men, and keep your expectations high.

Your kids need you. Your wife needs you. The world needs you to be the dad.

─────────────── **Takeaway** ───────────────

Grab a pencil and paper and ask your wife for ideas on how you can be a better dad.

> *"Your mother's encouragement takes away the fear of failure—*
> *affirming you have nothing to lose. Your father's encouragement*
> *creates a vision for victory—affirming you have everything to win."*
>
> JAY PAYLEITNER (1957–)

Wives Need Their Husbands…

To Let Her Be a
Stay-at-Home Mom

am not saying your wife needs to stay home with the kids.

What I am saying is that most new mothers have a God-given desire to hold and nurture their babies. Even if she loves her career, almost every new mommy has a very hard time severing her maternal ties to go back to work for six to ten hours every day. Sometimes the depth of feeling surprises them. Early in their pregnancy, they may have fully expected to take a three-month leave of absence and then jump right back into the old routine. But after holding their baby they just couldn't do it.

What I'm also saying is that if your wife really feels that way, it's your husbandly responsibility to do whatever it takes to permit that new mom to follow her instinct.

In other words, even if your wife makes a good buck, you need to have the discernment to recognize what's happening in her heart and the guts to say, "Don't worry. We can make it on one salary."

In other words, start planning early on. When you start making babies, try to be in a financial position where you're not depending on your wife's income.

What it might come down to is this: More important than a *big home* is for mom to *be home*.

Does that sound old-fashioned? It's not. It's very trendy. And it's very practical.

I am not going to do all the math. But I dare you to add up the cost of day care, transportation, business clothing, dry cleaning, lunches, fast-food dinners, and extra formula. That relatively simple exercise will help you realize that your wife's take-home pay isn't all making it home. Then add the expense of a few extra doctor visits because of the latest viruses fermenting at that day-care center. Then consider that your wife's income (which is mostly outgo) puts you in a higher tax bracket.

Beyond dollars and cents, there are all kinds of reasons for moms to stay home with the kids for most of their growing-up years. Feminist meddlers may as well save their breath. Even if that new mother has the perfect plan all worked out, it's impossible to argue with this simple truth: No one can take better care of a baby than that baby's mommy. How could they? No one loves that baby more than that baby's mommy.

Of course, every situation is different. You need to talk, pray, get wise counsel, and do what's best for your family. Maybe mom can work part time from home. Maybe Grandma or Aunt Sue would be thrilled to love on your little one a few times per week. Maybe dad (that's you) stays home. That's even trendier!

The point is, you need to really zero in and listen to your bride's emotions when it comes to this baby she carried inside her for nine months. You're the dad. But she's the mom. Until your new son or daughter is about a year old, her vote counts a little more than yours when it comes to childcare.

To summarize. I'm not telling you what to do. For my five kids, somehow Rita was able to stay home. And it worked. Sometimes money was tight and we didn't do a lot of big vacations. But we made it. What's more, I'm happy to report that Rita's sense of purpose and value didn't suffer. It flourished.

During the years she was "only a housewife," she did amazing things impacting thousands of lives for the better. She grew from classroom and church volunteer to PTO president for two different schools. Then to president of the high-school athletic booster club. Now she's an alderman for the City of St. Charles. (Which reduces me to mere arm candy, and I couldn't be more proud.)

Still, her favorite title, and one she wears well, is "stay-at-home mom for nearly 30 years."

Takeaway

The kids may never be able to put into words the sacrifices you make for them, but they will know you did.

"If you bungle raising your children, I don't think whatever else you do well matters very much."
Jacqueline Kennedy Onassis (1929–1994)

Wives Need Their Husbands...

To Heed the
Warnings of Proverbs 5

W ill you join me in reading Proverbs 5?

My son, pay attention to my wisdom,
turn your ear to my words of insight,
That you may maintain discretion
and your lips may preserve knowledge.
For the lips of the adulterous woman drip honey,
and her speech is smoother than oil;
but in the end she is bitter as gall,
sharp as a double-edged sword.
Her feet go down to death;
her steps lead straight to the grave.
She gives no thought to the way of life;
her paths wander aimlessly, but she does not know it.

Now then, my sons, listen to me;
do not turn aside from what I say.

Keep to a path far from her,
do not go near the door of her house,
lest you lose your honor to others
and your dignity to one who is cruel,
lest strangers feast on your wealth
and your toil enrich the house of another.
At the end of your life you will groan,
when your flesh and body are spent.
You will say, "How I hated discipline!

How my heart spurned correction!
I would not obey my teachers
or turn my ear to my instructors.
And I was soon in serious trouble
in the assembly of God's people."

Drink water from your own cistern,
running water from your own well.
Should your springs overflow in the streets,
your streams of water in the public squares?
Let them be yours alone,
never to be shared with strangers.
May your fountain be blessed,
and may you rejoice in the wife of your youth.
A loving doe, a graceful deer—
may her breasts satisfy you always,
may you ever be intoxicated with her love.
Why, my son, be intoxicated with another man's wife?
Why embrace the bosom of a wayward woman?

For your ways are in full view of the Lord,
and he examines all your paths.
The evil deeds of the wicked ensnare them;
the cords of their sins hold them fast.
For lack of discipline they will die,
led astray by their own great folly.

Don't be distracted by the poetic language or symbolism. It's really pretty straightforward. These words were written by Solomon, one of the smartest guys who ever lived, but you don't have to be a genius to understand what he's saying. Think of it as advice from an older guy who has made plenty of mistakes and wants to keep you and your family from ruin.

The first 12 lines are a warning about any and every kind of tempting female who may cross your path including prostitutes, neighbors, co-workers, your wife's friends, store clerks, and that cute receptionist at the dentist's office. Their words may draw you into suggestive or seemingly harmless conversation, but cross the line and you'll be cut into pieces. As a result, everyone and everything you care about will be destroyed.

The middle section gives you another dose of warnings, plus some advice.

You are reminded that even though *she* is doing the seduction, *you* have the ultimate responsibility to steer clear. Why? Because you have the most to lose. Your strength. Your reputation. Your cash. (Maybe in the form of bail, lawyer's fees, or alimony.)

The last two paragraphs suggest a better option. I hope you were paying enough attention in high-school English to remember metaphors and symbolism, because Proverbs 5 instructs you to drink your water from your own well and not overflow into the street. In case your skull is ridiculously thick, Solomon says it more straightforward than any passage in the entire Bible. "Rejoice in the wife of your youth…may her breasts satisfy you always, may you ever be intoxicated with her love."

Get that? Don't go looking for love in the streets. Rejoice in your own bride and…well, you get the idea. As a side note, if anyone asks whether or not you take the Bible literally, I encourage you to refer them to Proverbs 5:18-19.

Just before the last short paragraph comes the question "Why would you possibly hook up with someone to whom you are not married?" That's an excellent question, especially when much of the world is saying, "Why not?"

Finally, we are reminded that adultery not only destroys your relationship with your wife and family, it also holds you captive in full view of God, who designed sex to be a gift and blessing for married couples alone.

That's Proverbs 5. Don't turn the page until you've read it one more time.

Takeaway

When you read that short list of temptresses above—co-workers, friends, clerks, and so on—did someone come to mind? Steer clear. Keep to a path far from her. You've been warned.

"If the grass looks greener on the other side of the fence, it's because they take better care of it."
CECIL SELIG

Wives Need Their Husbands...

To Be on the Same Page When It Comes to Anniversary Gifts—Part 1

Show of hands. How many of you guys think that husbands and wives typically exchange presents on their anniversary? How many of you think that only the husband buys presents?

Logic tells me that spouses buy for each other. My wife tells me otherwise. In some families, apparently, tradition dictates that anniversary gift-giving is one way—husband to wife. That concept took me totally by surprise. What's really funny is that Rita and I didn't realize our different viewpoints until we had been married almost ten years.

Think about that for a second. Put yourself in my shoes. For our first nine anniversaries I listened for hints, checked the budget, shopped and wrapped in secret, and presented her with a more-or-less thoughtful gift. What did I get in return? Pretty much just a card, a kiss, and a thank-you. In truth, that's really all I needed. Hey, I'm terrible at opening presents anyway. And my needs are simple.

Looking back, gift-receiving during that decade was really just marked by some mild confusion and a twinge of annual disappointment. Rita had always been generous on Christmas, birthdays, Valentine's Day, even making me an Easter basket. During the year, she'd even buy or make me a gift for no reason at all. But—in my mind—she didn't feel the need to honor the day we were married.

I was never ticked off about this seemingly unfair balance of gift-giving, and it was never something we talked about. Finally, in a casual conversation, some married friends were talking about exchanging anniversary gifts, and

Rita was genuinely surprised that she bought a gift for him. That's when it all came clear. Our family traditions were different.

We laughed about it. We debated the issue, and the gift-giving has balanced out some. But it's still a little disproportionate. I'm not sure why. Maybe we'll have a little chat before next year.

So, husbands, if you haven't been getting any gifts on your anniversary, it might be because your wife truly thinks she doesn't owe you one. If that might be the case, talk it out. Get on the same page. And have a much happier and less confusing anniversary.

Takeaway

We bring all kinds of assumptions into marriage. Assumptions that may take a few anniversaries to figure out.

"When two people love each other, they don't look at each other, they look in the same direction."
GINGER ROGERS (1911–1995)

Wives Need Their Husbands…

To Be on the Same Page When It Comes to Anniversary Gifts—Part 2

I have been given clear instructions concerning anniversary gifts and from those instructions I rarely waver: something shiny.

The size and shape of the gold, silver, or platinum object(s) may fluctuate depending on the current state of finances or other priorities of our home and family. But I got the message early. Shiny is good. The shinier the better.

The best part about that mandate from early in our marriage is that I don't need to spend a lot of time extracting hints from my bride. Go to a relatively nice jewelry store and buy something within the budget and on sale, and she's happy. I married a great present-opener.

Guys, if you can somehow work out a similar arrangement, do it. Buying jewelry is easy. You're still surprising her, and that's important. But you're shopping at a place that's not embarrassing, and the clerks make it easy. Strangely enough, you'll soon discover that it's not the size or amount spent on that annual gift that matters. It really is the thought that counts. Plus, you don't even have to wrap it. That ring, necklace, bracelet, pair of earrings, pendant, broach, or pin probably comes in a nice box that the store clerks may even wrap for you. Include a card. (And don't just pick the first one you see. Stagger your card selection: funny one year—romantic the next.) In no time at all, you're covered for another year.

Now as a public service, I'd like to convey a short list of what not to buy your wife for your anniversary.

1. *A gym membership.* If your wife wants to tone up, slim down, and feel vibrant again, congratulations. But you cannot suggest, imply,

or hint about such a goal. You certainly can't buy it for her! You
even need to be careful encouraging her if she brings it up herself.
She may casually say, "I'm thinking about joining The Slim Gym.
What do you think?" The most you can say is, "Sounds like fun."

2. *A vacuum cleaner or food processor.* Yikes. Even if it's top of the
line. Even if she has talked about that particular model. Even if
she circled it in a brochure and left it on your nightstand, do not
buy your bride a household appliance for your anniversary. Neither should you buy a washboard, ironing board, butter churn,
or dish strainer.

3. *Sexy underwear.* I know you think it would be fun. But you're
walking in dangerous territory. What if it's too big? "How fat
do you think I am?" What if it's too small? She'll never wear it,
you'll never see it, and she will always wonder who you were
imagining when you bought it. Besides, everyone knows that
sexy underwear is a gift for you. And that's no gift at all.

4. *A beginner's cookbook.* You might as well say, "I think you're a
lousy cook."

5. *Cosmetic surgery.* Now there's a really bad idea. "Happy Anniversary, sweetheart. And by the way, I'm trading the real you in for a
better model."

Consider yourself warned.

If all else fails, and you really are at a loss as to what to buy, just ask. Tell
her you'd lasso the moon if you could, but you really just want her to be happy.

--- **Takeaway** ---

Women care much more about wedding anniversaries than men. Perhaps
it's because she needs to tell her friends the next day (or that night on Facebook) what you bought for her. No pressure there.

> *"I think men who have a pierced ear are better prepared for
> marriage. They've experienced pain and bought jewelry."*
> RITA RUDNER (1953–)

Wives Need Their Husbands…

To Never Repudiate the "Nose-Scrunch Rule"

(a.k.a. the "Across-the-Room-Wink Rule" or the "Mouthing-the-Words-'I-Love-You' Rule")

Like most married couples, you and your wife have a signal. You made it up by accident during one of those lovey-dovey moments early in your relationship. It's a nonverbal signal that works anytime or anyplace. Or at least it is supposed to work anytime or anyplace without exception.

You developed this instant undeniable nonverbal signal when you were at a family reunion, wedding reception, political rally, fraternity mixer, clambake, barbecue, town festival, church function, happy hour, tailgate party, museum fund-raiser, afternoon tea, birthday party, or some other social gathering. By that time, you had been dating a while and you had already courageously said, "I love you" to each other. At this gathering of between 4 and 4000 people you were happily socializing and pretending to enjoy the company of others. Across the parlor, park, or patio you and your future wife caught each other's eye and involuntarily held the gaze for several seconds.

In that moment, you both realized that you would much rather have been alone with each other. But you also realized that you might very well be together for the rest of your life. Then, one of you did it for the first time. It started with a little smile. Then, came the premiere transmission of your very own across-the-room nonverbal connector: a little nose scrunch, a wink, a very subtle kiss thrown with your lips only, a slight wave or hand gesture that no one else would even notice, or perhaps a nod and almost imperceptible eye twinkle. It could have been the words "I love you" said without sound and just the slightest lip movement. It could actually be a combination of the above or something that's so secret I can't even type it here.

And that's the point. It's a secret. Your secret. It's an exclusive trademark of your marriage. It says I love you. It says you are the most important person at this gathering. And you always will be.

Am I right about this? Do you and your bride have this signal in your relationship toolbox? My very informal poll suggests most married couples have signals they use across the room that say "I love you" and other communication tricks as well. When you're in close proximity, you have squeezes, brushes, footsie taps, whispers, eyebrow movements, and shared looks that speak volumes of love only to each other.

Well, here are three points to consider regarding those looks or touches that convey undying affection.

First, it's a beautiful thing. Speaking "I love you" has its own profundity and significance. But the ability to convey your love commitment in an instant through a crowd establishes a new level of intimacy. Don't take that gift lightly.

Second, if you have not yet established this communication resource, it might be because you never really had the chance. You never left each other's side at social gatherings. Or the moment just didn't present itself. Or maybe one of you is nearsighted so you could never lock eyes across a room. Not to worry. This is actually one of those cute little married-couple moments that you can create quite intentionally. You may think something like this needs to happen spontaneously, but you'd be wrong. Sometimes spontaneity needs a helping hand.

Here's what you can do. At your next social gathering, tell your bride she's looking especially lovely, make sure she's in good spirits, and then excuse yourself for a moment. Find a male accomplice, pick a point about 15 feet away from your bride directly in her line of sight, and then launch into a casual conversation, glancing regularly back to your bride. When she finally looks your way, lock eyes, tilt your head, smile, and use whatever means you choose to send a long-distance message that clearly communicates she matters more to you than anyone in the place. Wait a minute, then wander back and say, "You know, I was thinking that I'm so glad you married me. I'd be lost without you." Or something equally as corny. If it works, you've got a new way to connect with your bride that may pay long-term dividends for decades to come.

The third point is this. You are not allowed to break the contract. Once you and your sweetheart establish this touch point, it's an obligation you cannot mess with or deny. You may have never even spoken about it, but it's a binding contract as solid as your mortgage or last will and testament.

Let's say you and your bride have been fighting all day over something ridiculous, and it's the last thing you want to do, but you have to go to your Uncle Burt and Aunt Sally's fiftieth-wedding-anniversary hoopla. The 40-minute drive to the banquet hall cements the icy silence. Inside, guests are offering toasts and accolades to the happy couple. Someone tells a funny story about how Burt always loses to Sally in tennis. The same thing is true of you and your wife, and it's something you don't mind joking about. But this evening you're in no such mood. Your bride—touched by the same story—catches your eye from several feet away and delivers your signal. What do you do? Do you grimace back? Do you look away? Do you shake your head in disgust? Not at all. Your bride has taken the first step. You absolutely have to respond favorably. You swallow. Lower your eyes for a split second. Look back with just the slightest smile and return your secret signal.

No one else in the room knows what just happened. But honoring the signal is one of those secrets to a long and happy marriage. Just ask Burt and Sally.

Takeaway

FYI: I did not mention above the secret signal that I am privileged to share with Rita. Hey, it's a secret.

> *"Sometimes two people need to step apart*
> *and make a space between that each might see the other anew*
> *in a glance across a room or silhouetted against the moon."*
> ROBERT BRAULT (1938–)

Wives Need Their Husbands...
To Stay Married

The year is 1950. The Korean War begins. Charles Schulz introduces Charlie Brown to the world. Diners Club becomes the first credit card. The average new home costs $8500. It's the year of the first successful kidney transplant, the first dependable ballpoint pen, the first boxed cake mix, and the wedding of Marguerite Mauel and Kenneth Payleitner.

In 2010, my parents and the three generations that grew out of their love gathered to celebrate 60 years of marriage. We all went to church together in the morning, where Marge and Ken renewed their vows and then had a delightful brunch filled with toasts, shared memories, music, slide shows, and more.

In attendance were my brother, my two sisters, and me. Our four spouses. Eleven grandchildren. Plus, two more who married into that generation and others who would join the family soon. Adding an exclamation point to the day were two great-grandchildren, Cole and Rita Nelson, who will very likely have quite a few second cousins in the next couple of decades.

Some other folks were there—wonderful friends and relatives—but let's just focus on those individuals who would be listed below my parents in a family tree.

Consider for a moment what it means to these people I love so much that my parents got married, stayed married, and modeled spousal dedication for more than 60 years.

A recent study reveals that children of divorce are roughly twice as likely to see their own marriage end in divorce.* Conversely, any marriage that lasts six

---

* "Divorce begets divorce but not genetically," Indiana University press release, July 10, 2007, http://news info.iu.edu/news/page/normal/5982.html.

decades increases the odds of other marriages in the family going the distance. (These are not absolutes, of course, so please don't take anything for granted.)

Here's the point: What my mom and dad have done—literally—is to increase the chances that my kids will have long, successful marriages.

More specifically, my kids and their kids and their kids have a better chance of avoiding the well-documented devastating negative impact of divorce on families:*

- Children of divorced parents are roughly two times more likely to drop out of high school.

- Children of divorce are at a greater risk to experience injury, asthma, headaches, and speech defects.

- Teenagers in single-parent families and in blended families are three times more likely to need psychological help.

- Seventy percent of long-term prison inmates grew up in broken homes.

Again, these are not absolutes. But they do make you consider that there's some value to the concept of working on your marriage and staying together for the sake of the kids.

Moving beyond the negative impact, my parents and millions of other happily married seniors found young love and made it work. No doubt, they plowed through all kinds of travails and challenges, but the joys far outweighed the struggles. I hope you have a few of those older couples in your family and circles of friends to toast on their golden anniversaries and serve as models for you.

There's a great verse I love to quote in its entirety during my presentations to dads and husbands. It's Proverbs 5:18-19. "Rejoice in the wife of your youth...May you always be captivated by her love" (NLT). Because I don't want to distract you from the main point, I will not include what God's Word says

---

* Respectively: Sara McLanahan and Gary Sandefur, *Growing Up with a Single Parent: What Hurts, What Helps* (Cambridge, MA: Harvard University Press, 1994); Deborah A. Dawson, "Family Structure and Children's Health and Well-being: Data from the National Health Interview Survey on Child Health," *Journal of Marriage and the Family* 53 (1991): 573-584; Peter Hill, "Recent Advances in Selected Aspects of Adolescent Development," *Journal of Child Psychology and Psychiatry* 34 (January 1993): 69-99; Wade Horn and Andrew Bush, "Fathers, Marriage, and Welfare Reform," Hudson Institute Executive Briefing (Indianapolis, IN: Hudson Institute, 1997).

Wives Need Their Husbands...
To Small-Talk

One of the unfortunate aspects of writing a book for husbands is that my wife will read it and discover some of my secrets. One of those secrets is that I have a very low tolerance for small talk.

At social gatherings, I'm just not a chit-chat kind of guy. I know small talk is an American tradition. And I'm smart enough to get by. I have enough acting experience that I can even fake it for a while, pretending I care about the sustainable CO2 emission standards of your new Prius or the difficult choice you're making between tight-knot cedar or pressure-treated pine for the deck you're building. For me, when it comes to cars and decks my questions are simpler. Does the car start in the morning? Does the deck support my weight when I cross to get a pork chop off your grill?

(Dear Reader, just to confirm. If I have recently small-talked with you at a gathering, this is not referring to you. I was gripped by every word you said about the bocce ball tournament you organized last Labor Day.)

On the other hand, if the topic is something I care about, then count me in. Kids—especially my own. Marriage. My hometown. Book publishing trends. Advertising trends. Educational trends. Practical Christianity. But be warned, I have opinions. Which means the conversation is no longer small talk. It turns into a debate.

As a result I have very few choices at meaningless social gatherings. I find someone I care about and hunker down to talk about real things that really matter. I stroll from room to room smiling, nodding, and grazing hors d'oeuvres. If there are small children present, I goof with them. Or I play arm candy to my bride.

If you've ever been in a men's Bible study or couples group with me, you know that I won't let conversation stagnate into inconsequential small talk. If I get up at 6 a.m. to be there or give up a Friday night, I'm going to make it worth the while. I'll ask the tough questions or point out the elephant in the room and perhaps bring some discomfort to the participants. You may not like it, but—dang it—we're going to talk about things that matter and have life-altering implications.

Now this chapter isn't about me. It's about you and your wife. And there's a good chance, hubby, that you don't care much for small talk either. Which really might not be such a big deal unless chit-chat is one of your wife's favorite hobbies and she needs you to listen.

What to do when the idle chatter begins? You've got all kinds of options. First, don't treat her like a party guest from whom you want to escape. She will know and you will pay for it. When your eyes wander or glaze over, she'll sense it immediately and either sulk or get perturbed. That's lose-lose.

Second, look for tidbits of small talk that you do care about and ask follow-up questions in that area. For example, when she starts talking about the color of the bridesmaids' dresses at your niece's wedding, you can certainly ask if the groom's family still owns that fishing lodge. The conversation may divert from the story your bride was telling, but at least she knows you were listening.

Third, ask her permission to change the topic. Without blatantly saying that her story is mind-numbing, wait for the right moment to trim the sails and head a different direction. Instead, say something like, "Sweetheart, I'm sorry. My mind is in about sixteen different places right now. Something you said reminded me of next weekend. Is there something going on that I'm forgetting about?"

Done properly, the conversation will transition to something you actually care about: yourself. If the story she was telling is important, she'll get back to it eventually.

The fourth option, of course, is honesty. Which is in most cases an excellent option. You could say something like "Honey, this story you're telling me is just plain boring." But in this case, I don't recommend it. Not unless you really, really, really want silence. Two to three weeks of it.

So that's one of my little secrets that is not so secret anymore. I don't eagerly give or receive small talk.

But you know what? Rita already knew that. She knows just about all my secrets. And she knows all my husband tricks. I hope your wife knows yours. It's really for the best.

Probably the best way to respond to small talk is to enjoy the mindless break from real life. After all, our brides are just sharing the latest news from work, the beauty shop, Facebook, or the backyard fence because they want to spend some time with us.

Now don't you feel bad for wanting to get out of it?

―――――――――― **Takeaway** ――――――――――

The way women reach out to connect with their husbands is way different from the way husbands reach out to connect with their wives. Honor that.

"Life is made up, not of great sacrifices or duties, but of little things,
in which smiles, and kindnesses, and small obligations, given
habitually, are what win and preserve the heart and secure comfort."

HUMPHREY DAVY (1778–1829)

Wives Need Their Husbands...

To Know How to Recalfitrate the Centipular Febulometric Coupler Before the Tepstat Embulsifies

I made a huge mistake in our second house during our eleventh year of marriage. I finished our basement.

Framing the walls, electrical, drywall, trim, recessed lighting, two rooms, two closets, four doorways with hinged doors. I did it all myself except tape the drywall and install the carpet. It actually turned out pretty nice.

Looking back, my bride and I have decidedly different perspectives on my basement-finishing adventure. I think, *That was just way too much brainpower and physical work. What was I thinking? I'll never do anything like that again.* Rita thinks, *Jay is my handyman.*

Dear reader, let me clarify. I am not a handyman.

I dread any kind of leak, short circuit, or loose hinge. When the ceramic tile started pulling away from the wall in our shower, it took me six months before I got around to pulling down about 20 loose tiles, applying new adhesive, and regrouting the whole thing. Our screened porch and my bay window both suffer from extensive wood rot. My solution continues to be higher hedges and another coat of paint. Rather than properly care for a quality lawnmower, I buy the cheapest model available every two years. There's a fist-sized hole in the drywall going down our basement steps. It's camouflaged by a poster of Rae Anne's eighth-grade volleyball team, and I'm okay with that. Even as I ponder my next sentence, I can look up at the ceiling in my home office and see two plate-sized water spots caused by leaks from an upstairs bathroom. They've been there at least five years. I sure hope the ceiling doesn't cave in.

Got it? I could be handy. But I don't want to be. No excuses. No explanation. It just isn't how I'm wired. Excuse the pun.

More proof? I rewired a lamp last week and I'm pretty sure that counts as my big project for the year. Twice someone has offered me a free snow blower, but I've turned it down because it's easier to shovel than tinker with small combustion engines. I have actually turned down an invitation to bike ride with my kids because the chain was off my bike and it would be "too much work." Just look at my workbench and you'll see that I don't have the organizational skills necessary to be an effective handyman.

On the other hand, part of me kind of likes that my wife thinks I can do these things. It's nice to be needed. Maybe I do have some value around this rickety old shack. After all, she couldn't tell a cotter key from an eyebolt. Or a vise grip from channel-lock pliers. A shyster tradesman could probably even sell her a thermocouple for a garbage disposal or a condenser fan for a microwave. I would never be so fooled. Why yes, I am the man of the house! A master of home maintenance. Won't you join me in chest-thumping grunts of tool domination?

Sorry. Where was I? Oh yeah. Guys, sorry to say, it really is our responsibility to embrace our inner handyman. Change a lightbulb. Clean the gutters. Plunge the toilet. Replace the thermostat. Assemble the Ikea furniture. Wedge the sliding door back in the right track. And maybe even finish the basement.

In other words, if it's on the honey-do list, be a honey and do it.

Message to my kids: Despite the above paragraphs, this home-owning business is a good thing. Don't fear chasing the American Dream of settling onto your own piece of property in the suburbs. Yes, there's work to be done. But you're smart kids—you'll figure it out. If you get in a bind, I'll be right over with my toolbox.

Takeaway

If you come home one evening and your wife has taken it upon herself to tackle and complete two or three items that have been on your "things to do" for several weeks, you may have surrendered a small portion of your property rights and your manhood. You're glad the work is done, but it just feels like something isn't right.

*"One only needs two tools in life: WD-40 to make
things go, and duct tape to make them stop."*
G.M. WEILACHER

Wives Need Their Husbands...

To Get the Job
Done in the Bedroom

I am not inviting you into my bedroom. In these pages, there will be very little talk—if any—about specific sexual positions, frequency, pet names, and that kind of thing. Hey, it's private stuff. I don't tell my best friends this kind of stuff. So why would I tell the thousands of strangers who read this book? Plus, I am not going to do anything to spoil a good thing.

Now, I don't have to remind you of the importance of this part of your relationship. I also don't have to build the case that it's a significant point of conflict for some couples. But I do have to write this chapter. After all, this book promises to tell husbands how to give their wife what she needs.

So what does your wife need? I have no idea. But *she does*. And you need to figure out a communication method for communicating that need. Make sense?

Here are 24 possible ways to share ideas, concerns, and desires and open new doors with each other about the most intimate details of your life. Talk in short specific sentences about exactly what you would like. Talk in general terms about gentleness, patience, and love. Leave short notes. Leave long notes. Leave love notes. Text. Send e-mails. Talk over a quiet candlelit dinner. Talk in the car. Talk in the car on the way to a bed-and-breakfast. Talk during sex. Talk an hour before sex. Talk while cuddling after sex. Talk with a marriage counselor. Ask questions. Set limits. Give permission. Buy a book on sex from a Christian publisher and read it together out loud. Read it separately and leave yellow sticky notes at key passages. Listen to an audiobook together.*

---

* Appropriate books, videos, and audio resources are available at your local Christian retailer. See the end of this chapter for more information.

Buy candles, oils, lingerie, new sheets, or a new bed. Communicate with your eyes. Communicate with your hands. Communicate with your entire self.

Even with all these methods of sharing your heart, more times than you realize, the signals get crossed and communication gets scrambled. She's saying yes and you're hearing no. She's saying "this is great, now go slow and easy" and you're hearing "stop." You're doing everything you can to communicate "I will do anything for you" and all she thinks is you're being selfish. It's stunning how often couples who otherwise communicate very well totally misread sex signals.

There's frustration on both sides. Bruised egos. Hurt feelings. Tears. Anger. Sleepless nights. Lost opportunities. Lost marriages.

Please don't give up. Really, you're making this much harder than it has to be. At the right time and place, talk about it. First, laugh about it. Then, get serious. Set some ground rules or make some suggestions. Promise to trust each other. Then, kiss. Then, set a date night in the near future.

Still, don't be surprised. Months down the road, there will be another series of miscommunications and hurt feelings. Rules change. Expectations evolve. But now you're better prepared to interpret the signals and bring the crisis to an efficient resolution.

Finally, here's one last gift from me to you. Perhaps the idea of opening a dialogue about sex with your wife feels impossible. You don't know what to say or where to start. Well, blame this book. Really, it's okay. Use these words: "Sweetheart, you know that crazy book I'm reading about husbands and wives? Well, one chapter says I'm supposed to ask you if we should be doing something different in, you know, the bedroom. So...I'm asking."

Give her a chance. Don't interrupt. Let me know how she responds. On second thought, don't. Keep it between you and your bride.

Takeaway

One of the greatest rewards of a monogamous, lifelong relationship is making new discoveries and blazing new trails together.

"It doesn't matter what you do in the bedroom, as long as you don't do it in the street and frighten the horses."
MRS. PATRICK CAMPBELL (1865–1940)

BOOKS ON SEX

Sheet Music, Dr. Kevin Leman (Tyndale House, 2003)

Intended for Pleasure, Ed Wheat, MD, and Gaye Wheat (Revell, 1977)

Is That All He Thinks About?: How to Enjoy Great Sex with Your Husband, Marla Taviano (Harvest House, 2007)

The Purity Principle, Randy Alcorn (Multnomah, 2003)

Sex and the Supremacy of Christ, John Piper and Justin Taylor (Good News/ Crossway, 2005)

Red-Hot Monogamy, Bill and Pam Farrel (Harvest House, 2006)

Honey, I Don't Have a Headache Tonight, Sheila Wray Gregoire (Kregel, 2004)

A Celebration of Sex, Douglas Rosenau (Nelson Books, 2002)

Real Sex, Lauren F. Winner (Brazos, 2006)

Undressed: The Naked Truth About Love, Sex, and Dating, Jason Illian (FaithWords, 2006)

Love, Sex, and Lasting Relationships, Chip Ingram (Baker, 2003)

The 5 Sex Needs of Men & Women, Gary and Barbara Rosberg (Tyndale House, 2006)

The Way to Love Your Wife: Creating Greater Love and Passion in the Bedroom, Clifford and Joyce Penner (Tyndale House, 2007)

Recovering Biblical Manhood & Womanhood, John Piper and Wayne Grudem (Good News/Crossway, 1991)

What's the Difference?, John Piper (Good News/Crossway, 1990)

When Two Become One, Christopher and Rachel McCluskey (Revell, 2004)

Sexual Intimacy in Marriage, William Cutrer, MD, and Sandra Glahn (Kregel, 2001)

The Invisible Bond, Barbara Wilson (Multnomah, 2006)

Sex 101, Clifford and Joyce Penner (W Publishing Group, 2003)

Wives Need Their Husbands...

To Put Her Second

I f your bride is second on your priority list, who's on first? And no, this is not an Abbott and Costello routine.

If you said, "Well, of course, I'm the husband, so I'm first," then you haven't been paying attention. As a matter of fact, just close this book and give it to a friend who will enjoy it.

The answer, of course, is God needs to be first in your marriage and in your life. After all, he made you, knows exactly what you need, and wants to meet your every need. As a husband, one of your most basic needs is a close relationship with your bride. Would you agree?

Well, putting God first brings you and your bride closer together. An illustration I saw presented by a speaker years ago helped me tremendously to visualize this idea. Imagine a triangle with God at the top and a husband and wife at the two bottom corners. At the base of the triangle, they are miles apart. But the closer the man and woman get to God, the closer they are to each other.

Research confirms this idea. A 2008 study issued by the Center for Marriage and Families concluded that couples 18 to 55 who attend church services several times a month report happier marriages than those who rarely or never attend church.*

Even more compelling—and maybe surprising to you—is a study in the *Journal for the Scientific Study of Religion* that disproves a rumor that has been circulating for years. You have probably heard the conventional wisdom that the divorce rate is the same for Christians and non-believers. Well, that's just

---

* W. Bradford Wilcox, "Is Religion an Answer? Marriage, Fatherhood, and the Male Problematic," The Center for Marriage and Families, Research Brief No. 11, June 2008. (Commissioned by the National Fatherhood Initiative.)

not true. It turns out marriages in which both husband and wife attend church frequently are 2.4 times *less likely* to end in divorce than marriages in which neither spouse attends religious services.*

Notice the way the couples were described in those studies? They did more than just check off a box marked "Christian." The couples who experienced happier marriages and fewer divorces were active in practicing their faith. They actually got out of bed on Sunday morning and made it to church. Presumably, they also acknowledged God the other six days a week.

Ready for some "circular logic" to expand on this point? Strengthening your commitment to your wife gets you closer to God, which strengthens your commitment to your wife.

In the last book of the Old Testament, Malachi confronts the people of Jerusalem with their sinful ways and, in chapter 2, specifically describes how some men are crying out to God, but aren't getting the response they're hoping for.

> Here is another thing you do. You cover the LORD's altar with tears, weeping and groaning because he pays no attention to your offerings and doesn't accept them with pleasure. You cry out, "Why doesn't the LORD accept my worship?" I'll tell you why! Because the LORD witnessed the vows you and your wife made when you were young. But you have been unfaithful to her, though she remained your faithful partner, the wife of your marriage vows (Malachi 2:13-14 NLT).

See what's going on here? A bunch of guys who cheated on their wives can't figure out why God isn't answering their every prayer. In truth, God did answer. He's saying, "I was there at the wedding ceremony. Now invite me to the marriage. Only then will you have the joy you seek."

In the New Testament, Peter makes the point even clearer. He connects the way men treat their wives with how God receives their prayers.

> Husbands, in the same way be considerate as you live with your wives, and treat them with respect as the weaker partner and as heirs with you of the gracious gift of life, so that nothing will hinder your prayers (1 Peter 3:7).

---

* Vaughn R.A. Call and Tim B. Heaton, "Religious Influence on Marital Stability," *Journal for the Scientific Study of Religion 36,* no. 3 (September 1997): 382-392.

So how do you put God first? You already know the answer. Pray. Read your Bible. Worship. Get in a small group. Find a mentor.

But don't stop there. Rewrite that list so you're doing all those things *with* your bride. Pray with her daily. Get a couples' devotional and read the Bible together. Stand close in church and worship together. Join or start a couples' small group. Find an older Christian couple and draw on their wisdom and experience.

That's a lot to do. But harvest just a few of these ideas and imagine how fantastic your marriage will be one year from today. Yowza.

Takeaway

God was at your wedding. Now invite him to your marriage.

"Though one may be overpowered, two can defend themselves.
A cord of three strands is not quickly broken."
Ecclesiastes 4:12

Wives Need Their Husbands…

To Be Revolted by Porn

I'm going to try to write this chapter without being too graphic. But I still need the core principle to kick you in the teeth.

Let's start with general assumptions. When it comes to porn, most guys fall into one of five categories.

1. Guy number one has no moral standard at all. He does porn every day and there's no sense of shame or conscience. It's accepted and expected. He has, in fact, surrendered completely to evil. This short chapter will have zero influence on him. Yes, God can free him from the bondage of pornography, but these four pages will not even get his attention.

2. Number two is the guy who is in it just as deep. He has the same habits and knows all the same arguments as the first guy. He'll say things like "It's consenting adults making an honest living with other consenting adults. It's protected by free speech." But a voice—maybe the Holy Spirit—whispers to him repeatedly, *It's just not right.*

3. Guy number three feels remorse, shame, and regret, but still pursues pornographic images on a semiregular basis. He'll get in deep for a season. And then he'll get out. And then he'll go right back to it. It's a secret he carries. It's a burden he occasionally asks God to take from him. But he hasn't taken any personal responsibility for his choices.

4. Guy number four doesn't pursue porn. But when it finds him, he doesn't look away. He justifies it by saying, "Hey, it's not my

fault." Once a year a single issue of his favorite sports magazine has some swimsuit models—what's the big deal? Sometimes when he can't sleep, he'll scan late-night cable just to see what's on. And of course, doing online research he sometimes "accidentally" stumbles on to graphic images and videos. This guy is heading down a slippery slope. It's classic denial. And he represents many of the guys reading this book.

5. Guy number five has steeled himself against pornography. He has filters and friends in place to keep pornography at a distance. When he sees a female jogger, he averts his eyes. He has read *Every Man's Battle* and suggested it to other men. He would never touch a *Playboy* and almost never picks up a *Maxim* magazine. Any R-rated movie would have to be favorably reviewed before he would buy a ticket.

    Yet, guy number five is still in bondage. Even as he pushes pornography away, he still imagines what's in those magazines and movies. He's haunted by the images he knows they contain. Even if he never flips through a magazine or clicks through any XXX websites, he will use his God-given imagination to plug in images from the archive of naked women he has stored or created in the depths of his ensnared male mind. When honesty comes to the surface, he still is a victim of porn.

That's five guys. Five different types of men that none of us can judge or chastise. We need to leave that up to God.

Gentlemen, what we need to do is take care of our own business. The truth is, the guy we need to be is not on this list. All the men described above are still succumbing to the power of the flesh. They are drawn to pornography. They are attracted as if it's something they cannot live without. They may be attempting to fight it, but they are stuck using their own willpower, which is no match for Satan. In 1 Corinthians, Paul warns that we should not attempt to fight temptation on our own. We may think we're standing strong, but we're teetering over the edge of the cliff. Our only real hope is to look to God for a way out.

If you think you are standing firm, be careful that you don't fall! No temptation has overtaken you except what is common to mankind. And God is faithful; he will not let you be tempted beyond what you can bear. But when you are tempted, he will also provide a way out so that you can endure it (1 Corinthians 10:12-13).

With God's help we won't just back away from the fire, we will turn and run. We'll heed the biblical instruction to "flee sexual immorality." But what are we running *toward*? In his second letter to Timothy, Paul describes our new goal: "Flee the evil desires of youth and pursue righteousness, faith, love and peace, along with those who call on the Lord out of a pure heart" (2 Timothy 2:22).

That clear two-part instruction should be enough. Turn away from porn. Turn toward God. But we've heard it before and still we fall short. Very likely, we agree with the concept intellectually, but our human desires keep getting in the way. Sometimes we need a real-world reminder to help us take a truth that our head knows and turn into an emotion that our heart feels.

Here's that real-world connection. The young ladies in the photos and videos? Each one is designed by God for a noble purpose. She's a real person. She's somebody's daughter. Like every little girl, she had her share of hopes and dreams. Maybe she wanted to grow up to be a doctor, teacher, astronaut, actress, or athlete. She imagined her wedding day and pretended to be a mommy. Growing up, I can guarantee she didn't dream about taking her clothes off in front of a camera for an audience of thousands of selfish, sullen men around the world.

What happened to that little girl? Somehow she lost her way, lost all hope, and had nowhere else to turn. When real life comes crashing down on these women, their stories uncover a range of tragic circumstances including abuse, addiction, helplessness, homelessness, con artists, pimps, the lure of easy money, and the seduction of fame.

The victims are young women simply looking for love and meaning in their lives. At first their participation may be voluntary, but in a matter of weeks, months, or perhaps years, the hard-core reality hits. They're stricken with AIDS or some other STD, they witness the suicide of a friend in the industry, they are stunned by a phone call from a parent who knows, or they suffer abuse from a video producer who demands more and more degrading activities. I apologize for the mental images.

Are you repulsed yet? Sickened by the thought? The revulsion should come easily to anyone who has a daughter, granddaughter, niece, or goddaughter.

Men, don't settle for a life in which you constantly do battle against temptation. When the time is right, take a few minutes in prayer to really consider the horror and victims of the trillion-dollar pornography industry. Let it break your heart. Let it stir righteous anger. Then turn your back once and for all and flee to a life of faith, love, and peace.

Takeaway

Only Satan could take something so beautiful and turn it into something so wicked.

"If your eye causes you to stumble, gouge it out and throw it away. It is better for you to enter life with one eye than to have two eyes and be thrown into the fire of hell."

MATTHEW 18:9

Wives Need Their Husbands...

To Be Her Opposite

I'm not sure you should buy into the idea that "opposites attract."

Rita and I definitely are on the same page about most important life issues: where to live, how many kids to have and how to raise them, spiritual beliefs, tithing, vacation destinations, and so on. Believe me, it's a lot easier not having to debate or compromise over and over again on issues large and small.

We agreed on public school for our kids. But if I thought homeschooling was important and she didn't, we might have had some real conflict. When we left our old church tradition it was a difficult choice, but we made it together. We love our hometown of St. Charles, Illinois. It's where we met and fell in love, and neither of us feels called to move to the woods, the desert, the mountains, or the big city. For now.

If you were attracted to your opposite and married her, you might very well run into a constant stream of issues to work out. I urge you to approach your conflicts with mutual respect, common sense, united prayer, and big-picture thinking.

While many marital experts may encourage you to "seek compromise" whenever you face marital conflict, don't be surprised if often that is just not possible. If she wants to live in Orlando and he wants to live in Seattle, you could pull out a map and quickly see that Wichita is halfway. But it's not a compromise. If he wants to start a business and she wants to go to med school, opening a hospital supply store is also not a likely compromise.

On the other hand, being your bride's opposite has distinct advantages. You and your wife may delightfully, serendipitously fill in each other's gaps. The two of you may be real-life examples of that great line from the film *Jerry Maguire,* "You complete me."

Husbands, even if that's not exactly true, I recommend that you assess all your wife's gifts, strengths, and abilities and intentionally pick up where she leaves off. Be her opposite. Suddenly, the two of you are an unstoppable team.

Examples? If she's a spender, you need to be a saver. If she's a pack rat, you need to be a ruthless thrower-outer. If she's scatterbrained, you need to be a voice of reason. If she's a worrywart, you need to be a rock of confidence.

Suddenly her shortcomings are not cause for concern at all, nor are they a reason to judge, lecture, or begin divorce proceedings. The things she can't or won't do become opportunities for you to fill in her gaps. To complete the puzzle of marriage. To be a hero of sorts.

A word of caution. The best rescuers don't spend a lot of time talking about rescuing. They just rescue. They get the job done without pointing out how awesome they are. As a matter of fact, sometimes the person being rescued may not even know they were in danger. It's similar to when Superman straightens out a bent railroad track moments before the oblivious train passengers zip past. See if you can compensate for your bride's shortcomings and not make a big deal about it. Don't worry. She may not say it, but she will know what you're doing and appreciate you even more for it.

Looking back at the examples above. If she's a spender, go ahead and begin an automatic investment plan that takes out a chunk of savings before you even see your paycheck.

If she's a pack rat, encourage her to hang on to small items that are truly precious. But take photos of bigger items before they get trashed or donated to Goodwill. Items like that worn-out first sofa, funkadelic headboard, or beloved and chipped daisy canister set. A nice photo album of forever keepsakes will keep you from having to rent one of those not-so-cheap storage garages.

If she's scatterbrained, anticipate occasional misplaced items and forgotten facts. Keep an extra set of car keys handy and set up overdraft protection on your checking account. Include a reasonable time cushion and alternate plans in your daily routine. Use this phrase often, "No worries. It's all good."

If she's a worrywart, honor her areas of concern. Lead the family in prayer over the events of the coming day. Take heed of her premonitions about icy road conditions, identity theft, or kitchen-counter bacteria. Maybe she's right. Maybe you should slow down, shred sensitive documents, and invest in some Lysol with bleach.

Picking up where she leaves off is one of the reasons God designed marriage in the first place. Remember how he looked at Adam and said, "It is not good for the man to be alone. I will make a helper suitable for him" (Genesis 2:18). God knew that if you lived alone, you'd be stuck doing all this stuff yourself.

Oh yeah. Funny thing about this concept. You may think you're rescuing your bride when you fill in all those gaps. But all the while, she believes she's doing the same thing for you.

Takeaway

Applaud your similarities. They make life so much easier. Cheer your differences. They make life so much more interesting.

"In a good marriage each is the other's better half."
ALFRED HITCHCOCK (1889–1980)

Wives Need Their Husbands…

To Kiss Better and Kiss More

A short chapter to get you thinking about kissing.
Don't kiss your wife with nasty breath. What creates nasty breath? Smoking. Garlic. Onions. Belching. Cold and flu. Acid reflux. Gingivitis. Morning mouth. How do you know if you have nasty unkissable breath? Ask your bride. If she hesitates and says, "Well…sometimes," then thank her and do something about it. It's basic hygiene, good manners, and common sense.

Do kiss your wife anytime and anyplace. On her cheek. On her neck. On her forehead. In the kitchen. On the front porch. On steps. In the car. On a picnic. In the church lobby. In the supermarket aisle. In line at the amusement park. When she looks beautiful. When she doesn't.

Do look at her before you kiss her. Once in a while, hold her face gently in your hands and look at her for a full five seconds before kissing her.

Do kiss across the room. Secret blown kisses between a husband and wife create a nice way to connect during a busy wedding reception, family gathering, yard sale, or kid's birthday party.

Do kiss your wife in front of the kids. They need to know that passion is a viable option within the confines of a committed marriage relationship. Your kids don't see that often on TV. Scriptwriters and producers don't think married romance is interesting to viewers. Kissing your bride in plain sight builds a sense of security for your children in a world in which many of their peers have unstable family relationships. By the way, you know you're doing it right if your third-grader says, "Ewww" or your teenager says, "Get a room."

Don't kiss your wife only when you want something. If the only time you kiss her is in foreplay, then you are missing out on one of the great benefits of married life. You're also conditioning your wife to bristle at your kisses. She's

153

thinking about all the household chores that need to get done, and now she has to fight you off for the next two hours. That's not foreplay for her, that's work.

Do kiss her unselfishly. Make your kisses a frequent, loving gift delivered with absolutely no agenda, and she will soon learn to appreciate them, enjoy them, and kiss back with equal (or more) passion.

Keep practicing. Someday—perhaps decades from now—sex may not be an option. It could be for any number of physical conditions for you or your bride. And that's really okay. Because you have mastered the fine art of kissing.

Takeaway

It's good to think about kissing.

"You should be kissed and often and by someone who knows how."
Margaret Mitchell (1900-1949)
Spoken by Rhett Butler in Gone with the Wind

Wives Need Their Husbands…

To Surprise Her with Gifts

I recommend Gary Chapman's book *The Five Love Languages*. He doesn't need a plug from me—I think that book and its spin-offs have sold a gazillion copies. Still, if you haven't read it, put down this book and grab that one. It'll change your perspective on relationships. Go ahead. I'll wait.

Are you back? So did you figure out your wife's love language? Is it Words of Affirmation, Quality Time, Receiving Gifts, Acts of Service, or Physical Touch?

I am glad to say Chapman's book helped me quickly identify my bride's love language. It's receiving gifts. Which reminds me that I need to do better in that area.

Anyway. I don't want to oversimplify, and I do understand that all women are different. But it's very likely that gifts (of any size) mean much more to your bride than you imagine. Of course, the art of gifting takes high priority at the Big Five: Valentine's Day, Mother's Day, Christmas, your anniversary, and her birthday. But those are *obligatory* gift-giving dates. Please don't overlook the instant benefits of spontaneous surprise gifts.

Spur-of-the-moment gifts can be much more satisfying than Big Five gifts. Your wife may not say that out loud, but I'll bet she agrees. So here's the question: How often do we guys really bring home spur of the moment gifts—cards, flowers, candies, baubles, and jammies?

To repeat myself, I'm talking about gifts not connected to any holiday. I'm also not talking about a gift designed to get you out of the doghouse for some husbandly infraction. Neither am I talking about a gift that commemorates a milestone. (For example, when Rita passed on the gavel to close out her term as PTO President at Fox Ridge Elementary School, I gave her a tasteful framed watercolor print of a fox. I wrote a few words on the back and it still hangs in our living room.)

Husbands, you need a plan to give your bride a gift FOR NO REASON. Such a plan doesn't happen without some intentionality.

So here's what you do: Pull out your calendar for the year and find a month during which there is NO holiday, anniversary, or birthday. January might work. February is Valentine's Day. March won't work if your wife is Irish. April usually has Easter. May won't work because of Mother's Day. Are you following me? Every family calendar is different, but the idea is to find a window of opportunity during which to give your bride a "just because" gift. Mark that week on your calendar now. Write or type the words "Just Because" right in that date. And then casually surprise her on that predetermined date with a gift box or bouquet.

When she quizzically asks, "What's this for?" simply say, "Just because." You'll keep her guessing for days. And that can be a good thing.

Takeaway

Note to self: Rita's love language is gifts. Jay, do better at this!

"The manner of giving is worth more than the gift."
PIERRE CORNEILLE (1606–1684)

Wives Need Their Husbands...

To Trust Love

A re you afraid of falling out of love with your bride? Don't be. As a matter of fact, instead of being afraid, do just the opposite. Expect it. Anticipate it. Plan for it. Know that sometime down the road, if you haven't already, you're going to look at your wife and think, *Where's the love? Who is this person I'm married to? What's missing?*

As terrifying as that sounds, you need to trust love. Trust that in the very near future, the entire emotional tidal wave of feelings we equate with love will wash over you and your bride once again. And the fear will be gone. Until next time.

When the feeling comes that you are "falling out of love" the absolute worst thing you can do is panic. When you panic, you do things you regret later. You say things that hurt and, unfortunately, keep hurting your bride even after the gooshy love feelings come back. You start looking for love in the wrong places—from the Internet to the office party to the red-light district. You put up a barrier between yourself and the one person who also is afraid, who also wants to feel love again.

While panic brings trouble and regret, patience brings hope. Trust the power of love to do what it does best. Remember those verses about love from 1 Corinthians 13? We looked at them back in chapter 30 when we were trying so desperately to come up with a definition for love. Read them again, but this time see the passage as a promise.

> Love is patient, love is kind. It does not envy, it does not boast,
> it is not proud. It does not dishonor others, it is not self-seeking,
> it is not easily angered, it keeps no record of wrongs. Love does
> not delight in evil but rejoices with the truth. It always protects,

always trusts, always hopes, always perseveres. Love never fails (1 Corinthians 13:4-8).

Did you see it? Did you see that love has an inherent staying power?

You can trust love to protect and persevere. As long as you and your bride have not given up, love will not fail. It might not *feel* like it, but love is still there. It may feel like you're drifting further apart or stuck in some kind of desolate wasteland, but when you come out on the other side, love will be stronger, deeper, and more passionate than ever.

Taking one step back in order to take three steps forward is not unprecedented. The science of athletic training dictates that muscles must be broken down to come back stronger. Artists who have lost their passion go back to the basics of painting still life. Every year at spring training, coaches talk about working on fundamentals—throwing, discipline at the plate, making contact, practicing footwork, taking thousands of routine grounders. Veteran players look forward to starting from scratch each year.

So instead of panicking, consider going back to the basics. Spend time together. Do what friends do. Do what lovers do. Hold hands. Take walks. Talk it out. Remember the past. Envision the future. You didn't always love each other, but you grew into love.

There's a great quote from Anne Meara of the comedy team Stiller and Meara. She was responding to a question about her decades-long marriage to Jerry Stiller: "Was it love at first sight? It wasn't then—but it sure is now."

Your wedding vows were really a public commitment to trust love. In any given season—especially during the years when careers are being built and exhaustion rules the day—it may be difficult to even remember that feeling of first love. Be patient. There will come a time when you once again see your wife across a crowded room and your heart will say, *There she is. There's my love.*

---------------- **Takeaway** ----------------

Feeling in love is fantastic. Being in love is even better.

"One advantage of marriage , it seems to me, is that when you fall out of love with each other, it keeps you together until maybe you fall in love again."

JUDITH VIORST (1931–)

Wives Need Their Husbands...

To Sometimes Fix It, Even If It Ain't Broke

Our current home was in move-in condition when we moved in. The house was 20 years old, but it had been well-maintained. Sure, the wallpaper wasn't exactly our style. The Mediterranean hardware on the kitchen cabinets was a little much. The kids' bathroom had a blue toilet, but it flushed and didn't leak.

The one project that Rita wanted me to tackle right away was the rather large five-foot-by-six-foot fluorescent light fixture over the island in the kitchen. It had a contemporary lattice-style wood grille and sockets for a total of eight five-foot long fluorescent bulbs. It didn't bug me at all. I actually liked the way it illuminated the room. Rita did not agree. She called it the "surgery lights" and rarely allowed them to be turned on.

I heard her complaints. I validated her desires. And then I came up with a reasonable stalling tactic. I said, "When one of the bulbs burns out, we'll replace the whole thing." Funny thing about fluorescent bulbs. They last forever. Especially when the woman of the house doesn't allow any electricity to flow through them.

Nine years later they were still going strong. That was completely fine with me!

To her credit, Rita didn't nag. But she did remind.

My philosophy about home projects has always been that my bride will always have one for me. She has proven that over and over again. As soon as I complete one project, she finds another one. There's always another job in the job jar. So it's not like I can ever complete a task and find rest. All of which means one of the key motivators for finishing a project—well-deserved rest—isn't something I can even dream about. Living life without a project pending is not part of the Rita-and-Jay marriage formula.

So what happened to that larger-than-life light fixture Rita so desperately wanted to replace? Are you taking notes? It was a brilliant maneuver on my part.

That new fixture I had no desire to install became a fabulous anniversary present. I went down to the lighting supply store, grabbed a few brochures, and folded them inside a nice anniversary card. I didn't even have to wrap anything.

She opened the card, immediately knew what the brochures represented, and thanked me profusely. Within days we had picked out three reasonably priced pendant light fixtures, and I made a few calls that led me to a wonderful electrician who not only did a flawless installation, but also took down the old fluorescent monstrosity, hauled it away, patched the leftover anchor holes, and primed and painted the surrounding ceiling. All for less than I had paid for some more traditional anniversary presents in previous years. Did you catch all seven lessons I discovered quite by accident and shared in the above paragraphs?

1. When you buy a house, don't buy a fixer-upper.

2. When there's something your wife wants to have done, negotiate a reasonable delaying tactic.

3. Don't give in to nagging.

4. Spread out your home projects months apart.

5. If you can somehow replace a mandatory gift occasion with an optional work project, do it!

6. Find a good handyman you can trust.

7. Never do today what you can put off until tomorrow.

There may or may not be a legitimate lesson in there somewhere. But the real takeaway is this: There are things in your house or apartment that truly need fixing. Do those sooner rather than later. But there are also things in your house or apartment that are not broken, but your wife thinks they are. Don't argue. Don't debate. Don't put them off too long. And if you can kill two birds with one stone or take the easy way out, that's okay.

Gotta go. Rita wants to tell me what's next on her project list.

Takeaway

Every wife has a wish list. Every husband has a wish list. His needs to be the same as hers.

> *"The fellow that owns his own home is always*
> *just coming out of a hardware store."*
>
> KIN HUBBARD (1868–1930)

Wives Need Their Husbands...

To Make Them Beautiful

f your wife is ugly, it's your fault.

Let me be clear on that. I could make the case that we should always see our wives as beautiful. As a matter of fact, that's an ongoing theme throughout this book. Husbands need to look at the heart of our wives, where true beauty lives. We need to readily don our slightly out-of-focus love goggles. As the years unfold, we should choose to completely disregard a few grey hairs, a couple extra pounds, or some character lines in the corner of her eyes. After all, we ain't gettin' any younger ourselves.

The goal of "seeing your wife as beautiful" is totally legit. Can you say that's true for your marriage? Try this test. If your wife whom you love became scarred and disfigured in some tragic accident, would you still "see her as beautiful"? Gentlemen, that needs to be your frame of mind.

But that's not what this chapter is about.

I submit that you have the power and responsibility to *literally* make your wife beautiful. Beautiful to you. Beautiful to other men. Beautiful to herself—even when she looks in the mirror.

Here's how the principle works.

If your wife feels your unconditional love and support, she will walk a little taller and carry herself with dignity and confidence.

If you listen to her with intentionality and delight in the stories of her day, she will smile back. And her eyes will sparkle.

If together you take long walks through neighborhoods, pedal along bike paths, and dance at weddings, you'll both be a little healthier and a bit more toned and energetic.

If you take her to places where beauty thrives—museums, national parks, the seashore, gardens, cathedrals, theaters, art galleries—she'll carry off some of that beauty as she moves through the experience.

If you buy her flowers, she'll reflect their beauty for days even after their color fades.

Finally, if you create a nag-free home by studying your wife and meeting her needs, she will graciously maintain a gentle and quiet spirit. The Bible describes this woman as possessing true beauty that comes from within. A beauty that never fades and, by the way, has nothing to do with expensive haircuts, jewelry, or clothing.

> Your beauty should not come from outward adornment, such as elaborate hairstyles and the wearing of gold jewelry or fine clothes. Rather, it should be that of your inner self, the unfading beauty of a gentle and quiet spirit, which is of great worth in God's sight (1 Peter 3:3-4).

You have the power to make your wife beautiful. And I hope you do. I hope when you and your beautiful bride go out on the town, other couples turn to each other and say, "How did a schlub like that end up with such a hot wife?" If you happen to overhear those whispers, simply smile and feel free to take just a little bit of the credit.

Takeaway

If you see your wife as beautiful, she is.

> *"A husband's conviction that his wife is beautiful, or a wife's firm belief that her husband is courageous, to some extent creates the beauty or the courage. This is not so much a perception of something that already exists as a bringing into existence by belief."*
> ABRAHAM MASLOW (1908–1970)

Wives Need Their Husbands…

To Leave the Light On
When the Kids Move Out

My parents moved from Milwaukee to Geneva, Illinois, in 1952. They had four kids, who currently reside in Geneva, St. Charles, St. Charles, and Elburn. All within about eight miles. As I mentioned earlier, those four added spouses and produced 11 grandkids, three of whom are married. And the eldest grandkid has added two great-grandkids. Total: 26.

It's impossible to predict, but when the dust settles on this up and coming generation (all between the ages of 17 and 32), I'm betting that most of them don't go too far away for too long.

Now of course, I gotta be careful here. If one ends up in Seattle or California or Ohio or D.C. or even Peoria for a while, that's not a bad thing. In my mind, any location where one of those 11 young people and their spouses might settle instantly becomes a little better place. Maybe even a place worth visiting.

But the point I'm making—the reason for this chapter—is to remind husbands that as your nest empties, remember to leave the light on. Your bride knows this, but you might not. For some reason, fathers are more eager to hand their children a one-way ticket to get up, get out, and get on with their life. Dad, before that U-Haul leaves the driveway, I recommend you give your progeny one last hug and say, "Don't be a stranger. We love having you around." Or something like that.

Yes, your paternal goal for the first two decades of their lives is to have them move out and be successfully independent. But after that happens, the switch flips, and your goal is to have them move not too far and return for regular visits. Your wife wants them to come home, and you should too.

Where's home? Most likely, that's going to be the house your kids lived in when they went to high school. But maybe not. If you've been moving your family around the country because of career responsibilities, then moving back to your own favorite "hometown" might be the exact right thing to do.

No matter where you settle during this season of life, you'll want to consider a few key strategies. Don't wind up in some inaccessible location, unless it's an annual vacation destination like a hunting lodge or beachside paradise. On the other hand, don't move across the street. Make sure your new place has one nice big room that can accommodate your entire clan. Be a delightful destination. As your kids have kids, their schedules get busier, and their vacation time gets sucked up real fast. Don't guilt or nag your children and grandchildren into visiting you. Over time, that's a losing proposition. Instead, lure them. Keep the welcome mat out, the cabinets stocked, and the guest room inviting.

Coming home should be comfortable. For a weekend gathering, a week-long visit, or even a season of life, if that's the right thing for the right reason.

Even if you and your children experienced some strife as they grew, even if promises were broken or harsh words were said, you want to give your family every chance for reconciliation. How your grown children perceive that "home" might make all the difference.

Yes, we need to equip our kids to forge their own path and find their place in this world. Yes, we need them to build their own lives that impact their own corner of the world.

But it's just as important to give our adult children reason to say, "There's no place like home."

My parents must have done something right. The 26 of us have been through a lot. Ups and downs. Feast and famine. And we still can all go "home" and enjoy each other's company. That's a legacy I'm hoping to build for my own family.

I am also well aware that generational differences and cultural winds have blown many families all over the map. You may discover, Dad, that our most important role as patriarchs is to be intentional—and even obsessive—about keeping the porch light on and the welcome mat out for our kids and their kids and their kids.

For Christmas a few years ago, my daughter, Rae Anne, gave Rita a very cool plaque that now hangs above our front door: "Home is where your story begins." May I add that it's a story still being written?

Takeaway

Right now, you may be up to your armpits in diapers, Legos, science projects, bicycles, orthodontist appointments, or college applications. You may think your empty nest is light-years away. I suggest you start thinking about it now. For two reasons. It's good to plan ahead. And the dream of someday actually missing your kids may help during those times when you wish they would just go away.

> *"Anyone who does not provide for their relatives, and especially for their own household, has denied the faith and is worse than an unbeliever."*
>
> 1 Timothy 5:8

Wives Need Their Husbands...

To Anticipate the Dust and Drift

ave you ever been in a restaurant and, after a while, you realize that the
couple at the next table has not uttered a single word in the last 20 minutes? You're not eavesdropping because there's nothing to hear. The husband
unceremoniously breaks the silence by saying, "Pass the salt," and the wife
says, "Don't use too much." Then they go back to their expressionless meal.

The image is haunting. And very real. If I can make a grand sweeping gen-
eralization, the couple in this scenario are somewhere in their late 50s. The
kids are grown so there are no carpools, doctor's appointments, or afterschool
schedules to coordinate. Both husband and wife have compartmentalized
their life so that work stays at work. The household duties have been divided
years ago. Even hobbies, clubs, and church activities bring only the expected.
There are no new decisions to make. The routine has become routine.

Who would want to be that couple?

To be fair, maybe there's a reasonable explanation. They spent all day
battling bosses and deadlines, and they're just physically exhausted. They had
a big argument and going out to a public place for a quiet dinner is the first
step in getting back on track. They just dropped their youngest child off at
college or one of their parents off at a nursing home, and they're both lost in
their own deep thoughts. Silence is sometimes golden.

In truth, all we can do is speculate. Any couple at any bend in the relationship river might have their own reasons for experiencing emotional alone-
ness even when they are physically inches apart. Marriage manuals—which
this is not—are filled with pages devoted to healing couples who feel they
are "drifting apart."

What may cause such "drift"? It could very well be a product of spending so much time focusing on the needs of others that you forget to work on

your needs as a couple. Certainly there is a long season of life when your best energy goes into your kids, your house, your parents, your pets, your career, your neighbors, your church, your volunteer activities, and your other duties of the moment. There's no evil intent. It's just that when the dust settles on that season of life all you've got left to talk about is the dust.

So how do you get rid of the dust and the drift? An obvious answer is to launch vigorously into a new shared hobby—take tango lessons, join a book club, become AWANA leaders at church, buy twin jet skis, volunteer at the homeless shelter, wallpaper every room in the house, or just do anything that serves as a distraction from your apparent disconnection. That's one plan of attack. Truthfully, you can do a lot of good and have a lot of fun exploring these and a multitude of other options.

My vote is to not panic. Consider some pursuits that sound amusing to both of you, but don't go overboard or force the issue. More importantly, don't form an opinion about that couple in the restaurant too quickly.

Maybe we've got it all wrong.

Perhaps that picture of mutual isolation, the alienation that seems so obvious to us voyeurs at the next table, is just the opposite. Maybe the husband and wife who appear so cold and stoic are authentically enjoying a deeply satisfying moment of utter contentment being in each other's company. Maybe they've been investing in each other for so many years that they know exactly what each other needs. On this night, nearness, and nothing more, brings perfect fulfillment.

Any dust or drift has been swept away by a profound and unseen current of commitment and appreciation and a union of spirits. A quiet dinner may be the very picture of love.

Hmm. Maybe Rita and I do want to be that couple.

Takeaway

Cinematic love—loping toward each other in a wheat field, rowing across a lagoon, shouting from a balcony—is just a presumptuous precursor to authentic, timeless love.

> *"Love seems the swiftest, but it is the slowest of all growths. No man or woman really knows what perfect love is until they have been married a quarter of a century."*
>
> MARK TWAIN (1835–1910)

About the Author

Jay Payleitner is a dad. But he pays his mortgage and feeds his family working as a freelance writer, ad man, speaker, creativity trainer, and radio producer with credits including *Josh McDowell Radio*, *WordPower*, *Jesus Freaks Radio*, and *Today's Father with Carey Casey*. Jay served as the Executive Director for the Illinois Fatherhood Initiative and is a featured writer/blogger for the National Center for Fathering. He is the author of the bestselling *52 Things Kids Need from a Dad*, *365 Ways to Say "I Love You" to Your Kids*, *The One-Year Life Verse Devotional*, *40 Days to Your Best Life for Men*, and the acclaimed modern parable *Once Upon a Tandem*. Jay and his high-school sweetheart, Rita, have four sons, one daughter, and two daughters-in-law and live in St. Charles, Illinois. You can read his weekly dadblog at jaypayleitner.com.

The National Center for Fathering

We believe every child needs a dad they can count on. At the National Center for Fathering, we inspire and equip men to be the involved fathers, stepfathers, grandfathers, and father figures their children need.

The National Center was founded by Dr. Ken Canfield in 1990 as a non-profit scientific and education organization. Today, under the leadership of CEO Carey Casey, we continue to provide practical, research-based training and resources that reach more than one million dads annually.

We focus our work in four areas, all of which are described in detail at fathers.com:

Research. The Personal Fathering Profile, developed by a team of researchers led by Ken Canfield, and other ongoing research projects provide fresh insights for fathers and serve as benchmarks for evaluating the effectiveness of our programs and resources.

Training. Through Championship Fathering Experiences, Father-Daughter Summits, online training, small-group curricula, and train-the-trainer programs, we have equipped over 80,000 fathers and more than 1000 trainers to impact their own families and local communities.

Programs. The National Center provides leading edge, turnkey fathering programs, including WATCH D.O.G.S. (Dads Of Great Students), which involves dads in their children's education and is currently in more than 1300 schools in 36 states. Other programs include Fathering Court, which helps dads with significant child-support arrearages, and our annual Father of the Year Essay Contest.

Resources. Our website provides a wealth of resources for dads in nearly every fathering situation, many of them available free of charge. Dads who make a commitment to Championship Fathering receive a free weekly e-newsletter full of timely and practical tips on fathering. Today's Father, Carey Casey's daily radio program, airs on 600-plus stations. Listen to programs online or download podcasts at fathers.com/radio.

Make your commitment to Championship Fathering

Championship Fathering is an effort to change the culture for today's children and the children of coming generations. We're seeking to reach, teach, and unleash 6.5 million dads, creating a national movement of men who will commit to LOVE their children, COACH their children, MODEL for their children, ENCOURAGE other children, and ENLIST other dads to join the team. To make the Championship Fathering commitment, visit fathers.com/cf.

Also by Jay Payleitner

52 Things Kids Need from a Dad
What Fathers Can Do to Make a Lifelong Difference

Good news—you are already the perfect dad for your kids! Still, you know you can grow. In the pages of this bestseller, Jay Payleitner, veteran radio producer and dad of five, offers a bounty of inspiring and unexpected insights:

- *straightforward rules*: "carry photos of your kids," "Dad tucks in," and "kiss your wife in the kitchen"

- *candid advice that may be tough to hear*: "get right with your own dad," "throw out your porn," and "surrender control of the TV remote"

- *weird topics that at first seem absurd*: "buy Peeps," "spin a bucket over your head" and "rent a dolphin"

Surely, God—our heavenly Father—designed fatherhood to be a joy, a blessing, and a blast! *A great gift or men's group resource.*

365 Ways to Say "I Love You" to Your Kids

Expressions of love can get lost in the crush of carpools, diaper changes, homework, and afterschool activities. But Jay Payleitner is here to help you turn the dizzying array of activities into great memories. Learn to say "I love you"…

> …at bedtime…in the car…in different lan-
> guages…without words…doing chores…when
> your kids mess up big time…on vacation…using
> secret phrases…in crazy unexpected ways…in
> everyday life…in ways that point to God.

Whether your kids are newborn or college-bound, these 365 simple suggestions—from silly to serious—will help you lead your precious pack to joy, laughter, and connection one "I love you" at a time.

Other Helpful Resources from Harvest House

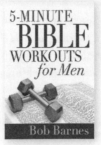

5-Minute Bible Workouts for Men
Bob Barnes

Is the pressure getting to you? Where can you turn to find relief?

With demands that constantly call for your attention, it's easy to skip out on your time with God.

If you'd like to change that, *5-Minute Bible Workouts for Men* is for you. Each devotion takes less than five minutes to read and offers valuable direction, wisdom, and encouragement that can strengthen you, your relationships, and your walk with God.

5-Minute Bible Workouts for Men is an excellent tool for maximizing your time with God. Start your day with a one-on-one workout with Him, and you'll be energized all day long.

52 Things Kids Need from a Mom
What Mothers Can Do to Make a Lifelong Difference
Angela Thomas

Angela Thomas, bestselling author and mother of four, draws on personal experience and biblical principles to help you raise healthy, responsible children and establish strong family ties. Whether you have one baby or six growing kids, insightful stories and practical information will bring you loads of encouragement. These quick-to-read chapters cover childhood through the teen years and are packed with specifics to help you...

- establish a positive, wholesome atmosphere at home
- make your children feel loved and secure
- teach and encourage communication
- know when and how to correct behavior and set consequences
- help your kids persevere and succeed

52 Things Kids Need from a Mom will help you discover God's wisdom for moms in a way that's upbeat and guilt-free!

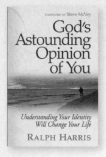

God's Astounding Opinion of You
Understanding Your Identity Will Change Your Life
Ralph Harris

Do you know that God's view of you is much greater than your own? Ralph Harris, founder and President of Life-Course Ministries, leads you to embrace the Scriptures' truth about what God thinks of you—that you are special to Him, blameless, and pure, and He respects and loves you.

With clear and simple explanations and examples, this resource will help you turn toward the friendship with God you were created for…a relationship in which you

- exchange fear and obligation for delight and devotion
- recognize the remarkable role and strength of the Holy Spirit in your daily life
- view your status as a *new creation* as the "new normal"—and live accordingly!

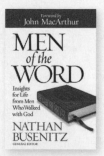

Men of the Word
Insights for Life from Men Who Walked with God
Nathan Busenitz, general editor

"A must-read for any man
who desires to grow in godliness."
JOHN MACARTHUR

What is God's calling for men? What character qualities does He value? What is biblical manhood, and how is it cultivated?

You'll find the answers to these all-important questions in the lives of the men of the Bible—men like Abraham, David, Nehemiah, Paul, and Timothy. Every one of them struggled with the same issues men like you face today. From them, you'll learn that real men…

- live by faith
- treasure God's Word
- pray with boldness
- flee temptation

- love to worship
- refuse to compromise
- lead with courage
- find satisfaction in God

Take the challenge to become all God wants you to be. His Word shows you the way. *Includes study guide.*